blue
rider
press

JACK'S WIFE FREDA

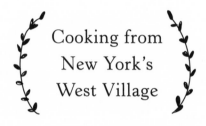

Cooking from
New York's
West Village

MAYA AND DEAN JANKELOWITZ
RECIPES BY JULIA JAKSIC

Blue Rider Press • New York

blue
rider
press

An imprint of Penguin Random House LLC
375 Hudson Street
New York, New York 10014

ISBN 9780399574863

Printed in China
1   3   5   7   9   10   8   6   4   2

Book design by Laureen Moyal, Paperwhite Studio

TO OUR SONS
NOAM AND BENNIE,
WHO MAKE EVERYTHING POSSIBLE

CONTENTS

INTRODUCTION

It's a balmy Friday night in June in Manhattan's Greenwich Village, and the glass doors of Jack's Wife Freda are opened to the street. From the soft glow of the restaurant, an energetic hum of chatter spills onto the sidewalk and encourages the crowd gathered there to wait just a little longer for a table. Inside, past the full banquets where carafes of rosé are ringed in condensation, past the small bar packed three bodies deep, co-owner Dean Jankelowitz swings open the double doors of the kitchen. "One more order of zucchini chips for table thirteen on the fly, brother!" he hollers to the expediter. The decibel level of his voice reflects the frenetic clamor in the kitchen—a good ten degrees hotter than the humid evening air outside. The three chefs on the line are working at Mach speed, a hand flipping a butterflied chicken as the skin crisps on the hot grill, a wrist flicking the handle of a panful of vegetables in a bubbling, spicy coconut curry. "You got it!" the expediter bellows over the din of the stoves.

Dean flies out of the kitchen moments later, handing off the zucchini to a server, "Table thirteen, seat two." She nods and weaves her way through the crowd with the precision of a ballerina.

Dean's wife and partner, Maya, is hovering over the stereo system, tinkering with the bass on a reggae beat. She carries an old-world sense of superstition with her. If the music is personal and the volume is just so, the songs will serve as a siren beckoning in a steady flow of diners—never mind that at 9:00 P.M. the place is packed to the gills and the wait is thirty minutes long. Waving hello with one hand and clutching a notepad in the other, Maya breezes back to the door to take the name of a new party hoping for a table, offering them a fresh mint lemonade while they wait.

Dean clears the plates from a family of four and suggests they split his favorite malva pudding for dessert. "What's malva?" the mother asks. "Oh, man, you have to try it. I'll send you one . . ." His voice trails off as he turns back toward the kitchen. Dean is a notorious mumbler but quick with a witty one-liner before vanishing to attend to another pressing task. The family seems momentarily confused—"Did you catch what he said?"—until Dean returns with four spoons and a sponge cake drizzled in warm caramel sauce. The kids' eyes go wide and Dean winks back.

By 1:00 A.M., the last satiated diners have sauntered out into the summer night. The chairs are stacked, the lights switched off, and the space is silent save for the purr of the wine refrigerators. Dean and Maya pull down the gate to the restaurant and walk past the noisy bars on Spring Street, past the weekend carousers stumbling on the Bowery, and head home to the Lower East Side. One can almost imagine that same path homeward about a century prior, when the neighborhood was the new home and refuge for hundreds of thousands of Jewish immigrants. Every other block housed a synagogue or a Yiddish theater. Families would have been asleep, stacked like sardines, in the tenements. And the pushcarts that held the vegetables, meats, and pickles that so many of those families ate during their Sabbath dinners earlier that evening were tied up for the night in the quiet downtown streets.

Food as an expression of familial love is one of the oldest and most universal of concepts, although the contemporary interpretation of "comfort food" has seized American culinary culture with a tight grip. In a country composed of so many immigrants, cuisines once thought of as colloquial in their land of origin are transformed into something exotic in the new American kitchen. Traditional dishes have been reshaped—fused, deconstructed, tailored to the New World palate while remaining rooted in the flavors of their native countries. In New York, perhaps no beloved food transplant embodies this concept more than Jewish cuisine.

Jack's Wife Freda, the pair of downtown cafés whose signs bear the illustrated face of their namesake grandma, is where Dean and Maya Jankelowitz have created a mecca of Jewish comfort-food dining. Both New York immigrants, they have managed to meld the Ashkenazi and Sephardic dishes of their respective childhoods with the twang and spices of South African and Israeli flavors. But the comforts of their restaurants aren't limited to food. Something in their detailed coziness makes them worth queuing up for and inspires diners to linger after the plates are cleared. Consummate hospitality serves as the bedrock of their

restaurants, and the communal, casual vibe feels oddly relaxed considering the flagship location is smack-dab in the middle of SoHo, one of the city's most kinetic neighborhoods. But there is a sense of traveling home when eating at Jack's Wife Freda, and it's no mistake that the restaurants are named after Dean's grandparents. Everyone has an origin story. Maya's and Dean's stories started some 6,000 miles apart and eventually converged in a love song to New York.

On a Friday afternoon in Killarney, a suburb of Johannesburg, the spring air carries the delicate honeyed perfume of the sugarbush, as the waning sun casts its last slanted rays of citrine warmth over the neighborhood. Inside Freda's kitchen there are wafts of sweet challah baking, simmering matzo ball soup, the snap of chicken schnitzel frying. It's the mid-eighties. We're in South Africa, and Friday afternoon in this predominantly Jewish neighborhood means one thing: the coming of Shabbat. Freda's ten-year-old grandson, Dean, is playing cards with his siblings in the living room and sneaking chocolates as family and friends gather by the minute. Freda emerges from the kitchen, her wig styled in a perfect bouffant and her arms covered in costume bangles, telling her husband, Jack, to fix her a cocktail. Their house fills with the raucous laughter of neighbors, arguments between cousins, and grandchildren shrieking as they play games in the yard. For some, hosting forty people any given night may be an overwhelming event, but for Jack and Freda it's a normal Shabbat—a familial comedy of errors, a delicious feast.

As the country headed toward the end of apartheid, political and racial tensions were at a steady boil in South Africa. Nelson Mandela had been imprisoned for nearly ten years by 1974, the year Dean was born, and apartheid wouldn't officially be over until Dean was twenty and living in the United States. But those decades, which stand as one of the worst scourges of racial discrimination, were the backdrop to Dean's upbringing in the very insular Jewish community in which he grew up. The circumstances that brought his family to South Africa date back to a mass Jewish migration from Lithuania beginning in the late nineteenth century in the wake of a massive gold rush. The Jewish population in South Africa had boomed from 4,000 to 40,000 by 1915. It was on the heels of this influx that fifteen-year-old Chaim Jankel, Dean's grandfather, was sent by his parents from Lithuania to escape the mounting anti-Semitism in pre–World War II Europe.

In 1925 Chaim naturalized to South Africa, taking the name Jack Jankelowitz. He joined uncles and aunts who had already immigrated, but his parents stayed behind to care for his grandfather. On Yom Kippur in 1940, his parents, along with the entire Jewish community in the town of Kruk, were marched out of their synagogue and murdered in the streets by the Lithuanian Guard. The lucky ones in the Jankelowitz clan who had immigrated to America and South Africa were spared the ensuing Holocaust. Perhaps eclipsed by the tenuous race relations of their new home, the Jewish communities in South Africa avoided the tragic fate of their European counterparts. And it was here that Jack met his wife, Freda.

Freda was native to South Africa. Her father, Charlie, was a homeopathic doctor who had fled the pogroms in Poland for refuge in England. While in London, he quickly fell in love with and wed a cockney beauty, Annie. The two immigrated to Johannesburg, where they raised their three daughters—Freda being the baby by fifteen years. She was only seven when her father died, leaving her mother to take over the household. Annie prided herself on being a true "balaboosta"—the Yiddish term for an excellent homemaker—and after the death of her husband she supported her daughters by monetizing her talents, cooking and baking for the back-alley card games she regularly held at her house. It was her mother's passion, and ease for entertaining, that Freda would, in time, lavish on her own family.

Jack and Freda married on January 5, 1942, in a huge celebration of family and friends during a warm South African summer. They raised two children, Anne (named for Freda's mother) and Brian, in the tight-knit diaspora of "Jewburg," and Brian and Anne would grow up to raise their families there as well.

Brian's son Dean was the second oldest of four siblings, and when Dean was six, his parents divorced. Jack and Freda became secondary caregivers to their grandchildren, and for the kids, it meant lots of happy playtime at their grandparents' home. Four young children can be a nightmare for a single working parent, but having a balaboosta for a mother is nothing short of a godsend. Freda would cook up a storm for her grandkids—cold borscht with sour cream, hot potato knaidlach, crispy chicken schnitzel, chicken soup with dill, chopped liver, chopped herring—the all-star lineup of Ashkenazi cooking. There was also *ptcha* (jellied calves feet), *gribenes*, *tzimmes*, and *kishke* (sausages stuffed with meat and matzo meal) from the Polish-Lithuanian Jewish tradition of making delicacies from the less desirable parts of the animal. In the face of scarcity, the flavors of Jewish cooking are marked with resourcefulness, love, and endurance. Jack would make potato latkes just like the ones his family had sold in Lithuania. Freda would fillet the sole as her mother had in London and bake her famous cheesecake, which never lasted long.

Freda was a quintessential housewife of the 1950s. Like her mother before her, she was uncompromising in the art of hosting and setting a lavishly welcoming table. She kept an impeccably stocked bar and bowls of treats and chocolate on every table. The quality and presentation of her glassware, silverware, and tablecloths were of the utmost importance, an impressive feat in 1980s South Africa. The United States and the United Kingdom had placed heavy trade sanctions on the country in an international protest of apartheid, so the simple act of making fried eggs with real butter, as Freda was known to do, was an extravagance. To Dean and his brothers and sisters, Jack and Freda's home was the land of plenty. "I think all our safe time was in that house," Dean remembers. "It was a very comforting place to be, filled with warmth and love and free of complication." It was a place without rules and no one wanted for anything, the children ever in the embrace of their adoring grandparents.

Jack and Freda passed away within months of each other, shortly after planning Dean's bar mitzvah. Their absence left a hole in the way of life for the family, knocking them out of thier comforting routine. Meals were increasingly eaten outside the home or cooked by African maids, immersing the kids in the regional tastes of South African cuisine.

South African food is a curious amalgamation of flavors, the result of centuries of imperialist government. The country's trade line through the Dutch East India Company brought various spices, such as nutmeg and curry from Malaysia. The influx of Indian labor in the nineteenth century came with chutneys and samosas. Mixed with both the native and supplanted agriculture, the result of these intermingling of flavors is robust, spicy, and never boring. Dean remembers the street food of his youth, the barbecued meaty *boerewors* sausages (from the Dutch, known as the Boerers, an Afrikaans word for farmer) flavored with coriander and nutmeg, the *mieliepap* served alongside (a maize-meal similar to polenta or grits—"pap" from the Dutch word for porridge—served in varying consistencies and made with sour milk). The maids cooked *potjies* (meat stews with potatoes and pumpkin) and the menu rotated

from day to day: fish on Monday, chicken on Tuesday, meat on Friday, and so on.

Dean's father, on the other hand, had a culinary repertoire that consisted of sandwiches and pasta. To his kids' relief, that meant practically all meals were eaten out on the town. A fancy Portuguese restaurant was a favorite, and there were plenty of decent Greek joints as well, but no restaurant was as beloved by the kids as Nando's. It was a casual restaurant with one very memorable specialty—peri peri chicken. Peri peri—or piri piri or pili pili—is the African bird's-eye chili, and simply means "pepper pepper" in Swahili. Nando's signature dish was butterflied grilled chicken slathered in a Portuguese-style peri peri sauce—ground chili peppers mixed with lemon juice and red bell peppers. The result was succulent, charred chicken with a spicy kick and just a tinge of sweetness to stave off the burning. The simmering warmth of dill in Freda's chicken soup and the searing heat of the bird's-eye chili, though not an obvious marriage, were influences that followed Dean across the Atlantic to New York in years to come.

Maya was born in upstate New York in 1978. The daughter of an Israeli mother and a Brooklyn-born father, she spent her youngest years moving up and down the northeastern United States, from New York to Delaware, from Philadelphia to New Jersey. But the connection to Israel was in the family genes. Her father, Michael, had immigrated (or "made aliyah," meaning "to ascend" in Hebrew) to Herzliya with his family as a teenager after the establishment of the Jewish state. He met Aviva while serving in the military, and shortly thereafter, they moved back to the States, where they had their own children. For Maya's family, their move back to the homeland, when she was eight years old, felt inevitable.

Like Dean, Maya's paternal line of ancestry came from the Eastern European Ashkenazi sect. Her grandmother Anne Marie grew up in the Black Forest of southwestern Germany, the daughter of a successful cigar manufacturer. In 1936, before the onset of World War II, her parents were able to procure a single travel permit for sixteen-year-old Anne Marie to seek refuge in England. Five years later, penniless and estranged from her family, her rabbi introduced her to Irving, a Jewish-American Air Force reconnaissance photographer stationed in London. That same rabbi married them in 1945 once the war had ended, and three months later, Irving's troop was sent back to the United States. For Anne Marie—as a German-born citizen—obtaining a visa to join her husband in America was nearly impossible during the aftermath of the war. Luckily for the newlyweds, Irving's commander happened to be Elliot Roosevelt, son of the sitting president of the United States. With the help of Eleanor Roosevelt, Anne Marie was reunited with her husband via a ticket on a chartered ship to Brooklyn seven months later. Maya remembers Anne Marie much like Dean remembers his grandma Freda. She was a well-educated woman who spoke French, English, Spanish, and Hebrew. She had impeccable taste and a penchant for presentation, and cooked all the Ashkenazi specialties for her grandchildren.

Aviva's parents were Sephardic Jews from Tripoli, Libya. They also made aliyah to Israel in the late 1940s when anti-Semitism in Tripoli peaked. Raphael and Buba ("doll" in Hebrew) were from large families and, in turn, made a large family of their own. Aviva was one of nine siblings. When Maya moved back to Israel as a child she was suddenly inundated by an enormous extended family, a welcome shock to the atomic family life she had been accustomed to in America. "In my memory, I grew up in very sterile Jewish community in a Jersey suburb," she recalls. "And then all of a sudden there was this warm, big family in Israel. My grandparents' home would be filled with uncles and aunts and about thirty cousins—and a lot of them were older so they had kids. The house was always filled with life, family, and food."

The cooking that came out of Buba's kitchen was as lavish as Freda's but different in style. Sephardic Jews cook with the spice and flavor now broadly associated with Middle Eastern cuisine. Buba cooked *shakshuka* (a spicy baked egg dish in tomato sauce) and *chreime* (fish stew with lemon and chili pepper), with the earthy flavors of thyme, oregano, and sumac in the za'atar that got sprinkled on everything. Not unlike Dean's memories of the *mieliepap* being prepared by the maids, Maya remembers, "Buba would make the couscous from scratch and there was a giant tub of it covered with towels that would sit overnight. And she was cooking for that whole family—around fifty people, with tables set up outside."

The Mizrachim (Sephardic Jews, specifically from North Africa or the Middle East) in Maya's family came from an old tradition of socializing that pivoted on family, community, and a dash of superstition. They considered themselves religious, though in a way that was more ritualistic than orthodox. They kept their house kosher according to Jewish tradition, but never required that their guests eat the same way. They observed Shabbat, but the television would be kept on—in case family were there who wanted to watch. Every quotidian event was a blessing or a curse, and either way, there was a passage from the Bible necessary to recite for protection: "The way they had of saying those mini blessings, and spitting out 'Hamsa, hamsa, hamsa' [akin to "knock on wood"—a Hebrew reference to the talisman that wards off the evil eye] made me feel safe. The grown-ups were always enforcing the good and shielding us from the evil."

The culture shock to young Maya was as alluring as it was disorienting. Already eight years old, she hadn't yet learned Hebrew, but deeply yearned to be part of its rich culture. She was surrounded by Israeli family and new Israeli friends but not quite Israeli herself. "I came from America where everything was shiny, packaged, and accessible. This was very different. It was the eighties in Israel. Israelis are so proud—they grew up with their foods, and markets, and kibbutzes, and their songs. I never felt like I fully belonged but I always wanted to. And I think being an outsider gave me this different perspective," a perspective that would eventually lead her back to New York to claim her Israeli identity on different soil.

Before she took that leap, however, she had to navigate the squall of adolescence, nearly capsized by her parents' divorce when she was seventeen. At that point in her life, itching to get away from the suburbs, she met her first boyfriend, a pilot in the Israeli air force. Maya was about to begin her own mandatory service and in the throes of first love, she found a trusted confidant and a glimpse at the world outside her family's scope. "I moved into the apartment he rented—the cutest little apartment in the center of Tel Aviv. And that's when I learned that

there's a world out there, and you can create your own world, and break your own pattern and start your own thing." In Tel Aviv, Maya had the revelation that the electric pace and mottled diversity of city life suited her.

Maya survived her army service but her relationship did not. She moved into an apartment of her own and took short-lived gigs working in the service industry— behind the counter of a Burger Ranch, waiting tables at a Japanese restaurant run by Filipinos. Eventually she halfheartedly settled into a job at the airport but by then the initial luster of living in Tel Aviv had worn thin. She spent her hours daydreaming about the far-flung destinations stamped on the passports she saw every day. "Working in the airport, I always had this underlying hunger to escape: being around different people, tasting different cultures, this idea of going into the unknown." With an aimless future weighing on her, she set her anxious eyes on a trip to the United States. It was an easy choice—her American passport would allow her to look for work—and though she was traveling alone she worked up the nerve to buy a round-trip ticket to New York.

Both Maya and Dean describe their rambling days getting situated in America similarly. Neither had any seed money nor a clue as to what they would do once they were here. Neither had close friends to show them the ropes. They had bought return tickets back to their home countries, but neither ended up using them. Dean kept the ticket folded in his wallet for years, a prized token of immigrant grit and autonomy.

Dressed in cutoffs and wearing a bandanna on his head, twenty-year-old Dean arrived in New York the summer of 1994. He dropped his bags off at the Harlem YMCA and sauntered downtown to Central Park. "My love affair with America was so huge—I grew up watching *Dallas* and *The Jazz Singer* with Neil Diamond. And I remember there was a movie called *The Prince of Central Park*, about a kid who lived in the park. That was how I felt—very free. During apartheid we were so closed off to everything. So the more you see, the more you want to see." Six years later, Maya had the same feeling of novelty and elation when she got off a plane on a very cold December night. "My best friend knew a guy we went to high school with who lived in Forest Hills, which sounded so magical to me. When I got off the plane, I took a train to a bus and just went there. It was winter and there were Christmas trees everywhere and I thought it was incredible. And then I arrived at this little one-bedroom apartment in Queens with four Israelis living there. But I felt so lucky!"

Like so many immigrants before them, Dean and Maya were initially buoyed up by strangers who had made the same journey. Maya was immediately hired by an Israeli at a retail store in SoHo. During her lunch break one day, she stumbled into the grand French brasserie Balthazar around the corner, entirely unaware of owner Keith McNally's booming popularity in the New York restaurant scene. She was even more oblivious to the fact that she would meet her future husband, the father of her children, and her eventual business partner there. Coffee cup in hand, she surveyed the place and was impressed by its scale and affable charm. She inquired about a job, and they hired her as a hostess the following week.

Dean had a somewhat less linear journey. He lived at the YMCA for two months before he had burned through most of his cash, so he used a portion of his dwindling funds to book a flight to Houston, Texas, to stay with a South African uncle. An ill-advised three-day layover in Las Vegas succeeded in hammering the nail in his bank account's coffin, "I remember getting off the plane and needing to call him and I didn't have any money—I think I had two quarters. I had to call him collect from the airport to come get me." In Houston, Dean set to work waiting tables—as he'd done since his teenage years—and lived with his uncle until he saved enough to go stay with a cousin in San Diego. A neighbor there hooked him up with a flight attendant job. He flew with a private airline between Los Angeles and New York and enjoyed being a fly on the wall when Bob Dole was on the presidential campaign trail, or while Norman Mailer quietly perused a copy of *Fear and Loathing in Las Vegas*, or when the Chicago Bulls packed the plane between games. Flying back and forth over the United States was exactly the kind of job that appealed to Dean, still unsure where to land. He stuck with it for two years before he felt the magnetism of New York pulling him back again.

Dean floated around the restaurant scene in the late '90s. He was hired as a waiter at Pastis (Balthazar's sister restaurant in the Meatpacking District) despite showing up on his first day of work with stitches in his chin and a black eye, remnants of his twenty-fifth birthday party, of which he remembers very little. It was perhaps the best kind of testament to the energy of downtown New York in that era. Bleecker Street was still lined with head shops and tattoo parlors below Washington Square Park. Antiques stores and first-edition bookshops were in the West Village. Magnolia Bakery was a quaint neighborhood cupcake place staffed by surly NYU students, and the Meatpacking District, though gentrifying rapidly, was still home to a bevy of nighttime characters, jazz musicians who played secret shows in derelict buildings, and the beautiful kaleidoscopic eccentrics who spilled out of the after-hours eatery Florent from dusk till dawn. It had the precise cultural intermingling that eventually causes a neighborhood to implode, pricing out the artistic inhabitants who have created it. But at that moment, it was also the reason why showing up with a busted chin wasn't an employment deal-breaker for Dean.

By the autumn of 2001, life had been an exhilarating blur of a party for him, hopping between restaurant jobs and working on documentaries. All of that came to an abrupt halt on September 11. Dean had been living on Greenwich Street, a few blocks from the World Trade Center, for about two years. On that day his apartment building fell victim to the towers. "It was a disaster in my personal life. Everything just kind of crumbled. I was out and working and partying all the time, having a lot of fun in the city. And then all of a sudden I had no home the next day." He moved in with his girlfriend and quit his job at Pastis, understandably favoring the tranquility of uptown compared to all he had lost downtown. The hiatus served its purpose of helping him to move on from the trauma and eventually stirring within him the urge to start anew. A year later he rented an apartment on the Lower East Side and called Keith McNally to ask for a job again. "Keith said, 'Great, we're opening this new place, Schiller's, in a few months.' And I said, 'That sounds fantastic but I need a job, like, right now.' And he said, 'Well, fine. Go be a breakfast waiter at Balthazar.' And I said, 'That sounds amazing!' And it was. Because that was where I met Maya."

Four years after she left Israel and began working at Balthazar, Maya had carved out a charmed life for herself in the East Village, and though she could barely afford the $800 rent, she found support in friends, mentors, and an array of creatives struggling to make it on their own. She was assiduous, pulling five to six shifts a week at the restaurant, first as a hostess, then as a coat checker, a waiter, eventually moving up the ranks to maître d'— all while working her way through graphic design school at night. "I was just so happy to work, to create my own life—and I was good at it. I realized working in the service business, people had outside dreams or aspirations but I took the job really seriously and felt that I was part of something. There was always this distant thought that I was going to have to go back home—but the energy of downtown New York City made me feel something new, made me want to commit and stay. It was the first time I felt like my life was becoming my own. It felt like a miracle." Though she had to consign old dresses in order to eat breakfast, and sell her paintings as "affordable art" for subway fare, this new independence liberated her. She had discovered a sense of self and place. "I was listening to music, taking pictures, and painting all day—I felt like an artist. And I have these memories of being lonely and broke and struggling— but now when I think about being in my twenties in the city, I think: I'm so lucky that I had that! I was all alone and had nothing, but it felt like so much. It was just like the whole world opened up."

This was the Maya Dean immediately fell in love with when he took the job at Balthazar. His father testifies to getting a phone call from Dean saying, "I met my future wife. She's Israeli. I'm too scared to go within four feet of her so I have to stay away." For Maya, it took a bit longer to come around—partly due to the fact that Dean acted literally on his fear, standing four feet away from the hostess podium, performing elaborate pantomimes in hopes of getting her attention. Like some unhinged version of Buster Keaton, Dean would strut within her sight line, producing an imagined paintbrush out of his pressed floor-length apron. After a long drag off his pretend cigarette, he would furiously splatter color onto a make-believe canvas—a bizarre courtship charade in which Jackson Pollock wins Maya's heart. "The Russian hostess next to me would say, 'He's so strange. Tell him to go away!'" She laughs in recollection. "I thought he was completely insane."

Of course, Dean eventually bridged the four-foot gap and Maya discovered that she liked the weirdo. They met in Tompkins Square Park for their first date, amid the burnt-out hippies, downtown misfits, and tweaking junkies. A shambling jazz band provided the score. Dean texted Maya: *Find me by the out-of-tune flute.* To this day, he'll text her the same thing when they're looking for each other in a crowd. They talked until daybreak in her apartment. The following day Dean moved in with Maya and never left.

In retrospect, theirs is a love story that seems equal parts improbable and inevitable. The distances they had to travel to find each other, the circumstances that had to align, the discouraging example set by the failed marriages of their parents . . . and yet, Dean and Maya shared a deep understanding of what family meant to them. Their happiest memories were cemented by the love of strong family matriarchs, and both had still chosen to branch off from the security of their families in pursuit of their own selfhood.

Dean bought an engagement ring in January 2004, two days before his birthday. He liked the feeling of carrying it around in his pocket, not really sure how to propose or where to do it. He and Maya had a birthday lunch, as usual, at a Moroccan café where they ate half their meals. Dean slid the ring across the table, and they spent the rest of the day celebrating in a flurry of champagne and friends. Four months later they recited their vows in Jerusalem on a balcony overlooking the Western Wall, under a South African chuppah.

When Schiller's Liquor Bar opened on the Lower East Side, it attracted the young, pretty downtown kids like flies to honey. It was an instant success with its sexy candlelit incandescence, the roar of patrons ping-ponging off the tiled walls. People stumbled down a staircase to the communal bathrooms, washing their hands at the center island trough—across which flirtatious glances nearly negated the act of hand cleaning. The let-down-your-hair, unbuttoned atmosphere was in no small part due to Dean's orchestration. Under his management, regular customers were greeted by nicknames Dean made up, heralded by the round of applause he would initiate with, "So-and-so just entered the building, ladies and gentlemen!" He would send desserts with enormous sparklers ablaze to an unsuspecting birthday-less group of girls. He would send shots to single people sitting next to each other at the bar, shamelessly introducing them. He'd send a round of cheap tequila to noisy frat boys, knowing it would be easier to oust them if they thought of him as one of the brothers. In truth, everyone was dubbed "brother" by him, and it bred a communal party that made you want to laugh with strangers and spend whatever was in your wallet until he kicked you out at closing.

Maya wielded the same influence, albeit to a more grown-up crowd, at Balthazar. It was, and remains, an institution in the New York dining scene, known for its classic French café menu and attentive service. A varied set of celebrities, regulars, and tourists—all of whom had high standards and expectations—came through the door. Perhaps it's the balaboosta in her bloodline, but Maya knew exactly how to read what a person needed in order to feel welcomed and accommodated. She knew that the mother with the stroller didn't have patience to wait long for her kid to eat, so crayons appeared as soon as they were seated. She could sense that the surly European man coming straight from the airport needed a drink on the house to soften the wait for his reservation. For the highly visible fashion magazine editor, a favorite table had better be ready when she arrived. Like an expert tailor, every customer's comfort measurements were different, but Maya could guess them at a glance with startling accuracy. Dean is well acquainted with these qualities in his wife: "Maya's energy on the floor is the best in the city. Her care for customers and the staff is so deep, and that's really all a restaurant is: caring for the people who work with you and the people who come inside."

It is no wonder, then, that this couple with their respective instincts for hospitality would eventually come to open their own restaurant. When their first son, Noam, was born, both were struck with a sense of restlessness, and a feeling that they couldn't keep working late shift hours with their baby at home. Once Noam was old enough to go to school, Dean would never see him if he was managing a bar all night. For Maya, too, there was an ache for a new maturity and evolution in their lives. "I remember when we had our two days off we loved to walk around, go to restaurants, the movies, the museums, dance and enjoy ourselves. We would just meander the neighborhoods and smoke cigarettes and love the city. And then we had the baby, and we were doing pretty much the same thing but pushing a stroller." It took four years and a second pregnancy for them to take the leap to ownership, but during that time the idea had taken root and nagged at them. "When you look at the immigrant story from South Africa, people always had their own businesses," Dean reflects. "They weren't part of a huge commercial culture. You worked hard and you developed your own trade. It's an immigrant feeling and it's part of Jewish identity—there's something about having your own business that has always felt truthful. Your name is who you are. This business is who we are."

Noam's little brother, Bennie, was born in the spring of 2011, and by early October Maya and Dean had signed a lease for their restaurant at 224 Lafayette Street.

With an infant and toddler in tow, they drew every last dollar out of their savings account to pay the key money for the business. They had forged countless friendships with fellow downtowners over the years, had expertise in the area's varied customer base, and were emotionally invested in the community. In return, the whole neighborhood (and then some) eventually showed up to eat. At that point they still were not sure of the kind of restaurant they wanted to own, or what they would name it. "We were going to call it Alfred's—for no reason. Because it looked polite or vanilla or buttoned-up or something." Jack's Wife Freda was a funny harebrained idea Dean had thrown around months earlier—one that was met with a great deal of outside resistance. "They said that no one would invest in a restaurant with that ridiculous name," Maya said. But similar to the location, Freda's name was synonymous with hospitality, and though Maya had never had the chance to meet her, she felt a strong connection with the balaboosta grandmother Dean held so dear. Jack's Wife Freda had a ring of casual familiarity to it—the suggestion of eating in your grandparents' or friend's home—and it squared nicely with their sense of belonging in the SoHo neighborhood. "We thought the name was funny," says Dean, "but it also had spiritual importance that was grounded in family. This idea with wine, terroir—where the soil, the sand, the sun, the love, the hill, the house—everything has a meaning in the taste of the wine. So once we had the name, it felt like everything found its purpose. And all the things we sourced for Lafayette came from within a mile of the place, whether it was the banquettes, the tables, the chairs, the lights. We were committing to the city and to our lives here. We loved the city so much and wanted to give back to it, to be part of it, and make our history part of it too."

The three months before opening are remembered in a haze of construction, design, and fortitude. They pooled beloved friends and family together as investors. The laundry list of things to complete, orders to make, and banquettes to measure left little space for doubt. But the front of the house found its conceptual groove: an approachable café, the kind they had loved in Paris and Tel Aviv and in their favorite downtown restaurants. "We wanted a place with long hours, where you can sit and have a cup of coffee, where you're welcome to celebrate your birthday or bring your family, and where there's always a warm reception when you walk in." They wanted to foster a sense of recognition among their guests—not demographically, but rather a sharing of sensibility and belonging, "a place where you feel like you're part of something, of the neighborhood, of the background. The kind of place where you always know someone in the room. Maybe someone you've seen on the block or at another restaurant, or you worked with them, or a friend has. A familiar feeling—that you know you're in the right place because there are like-minded people around." These elements had gone into every detail of assembly, from the intimate three-seat marble bar to the kitschy porcelain koi fish sugar cups. Implausibly, there was one rather essential component to the restaurant that had not yet been settled: the menu.

Maya and Dean had been auditioning chefs for the job but nothing had stuck. The food they were tasting, though delicious, was off the mark—too fussy or pretty or ego-driven.

An Israeli baker friend had been present for the first series of unsuccessful tastings and heard their discomfort with the buttery food, the suggestion of bacon on the menu, the complicated recipes. She advised them to make a list of all the things they liked and to take it from there. Dean and Maya had been so at ease with the front of house that they had overestimated their ability to engineer what came out the kitchen. They sat down that night and began listing the foods that told their story. They talked about the croque madame they had on their honeymoon in Paris, the soft-boiled eggs they cracked together for breakfast, the fresh mint "Nana" teas they drank in sidewalk cafés in Tel Aviv. Dean called his brother and reminisced about the peri peri chicken and prego steak sandwiches at Nando's. They added Grandma Freda's matzo ball soup and her salads and sweetbreads. Maya wanted Buba's couscous and shakshuka on the list. Together they filled the menu with the tastes that had nourished them in their childhoods and reminded them of the generosity of their families, flavors they wanted their two boys to grow up tasting. They were meals they had shared while traveling together and the food that had sustained them while falling in love with one another and the city. When they met Julia just two weeks before opening, Dean took this patchwork list out of his pocket and showed it to her. "She literally went down the list and said, 'Great! I can do that, I can do that. Yes, I can make this for you!'

And that's how the menu came along. Julia took everything we loved and made it make sense."

Jack's Wife Freda opened its doors on Friday, January 13, 2012. For Jews, the number 13 is lucky and Shabbat is holy, and as it turned out, that date brought all the holy luck they hoped it would. Soon glowing reviews were being written and photographs of the colorful food were widely circulated. Word of this restaurant with the funny name spread at a pace they could just barely keep up with. But sheer luck wasn't enough. In truth, the lasting success of Jack's Wife Freda was hard earned. The restaurant became a living, breathing thing—like a third child—one that needed constant care and attention. "When we opened, we were each like an octopus with eight arms doing it ourselves," Maya recalls with angst. "Nothing just happened on its own and everything was important: the ripeness of the avocados, if the bathroom wasn't cleaned, if the WiFi went down. Dean was hovering there like a hawk—waiting for a problem to arise so he could be there to fix it." When the security gate broke at two o'clock in the morning, Dean sat out front waiting for someone to show up to fix it at five. During brunch, Maya greeted guests at the door with baby Bennie strapped to her chest. When the dishwasher broke midshift and none of the repair services showed, Dean rolled up his sleeves and washed plates alongside the kitchen staff.

But from the get-go, former coworkers and loyal friends showed up at Jack's Wife Freda in droves, eager to pitch in and get things up and running. Trained in the same sensibilities as Maya and Dean, staff members worked in the trenches when they first got busy, and then became slammed. Their team still has that same multitasking gusto that was necessary in the early days; it's not uncommon to find a manager taking orders, servers bussing and setting tables, or an expediter running food from inside the kitchen and picking up empty plates on the way back. Enthusiastic and inspired, it's as if everyone in their battalion of employees grew the same set of octopus arms.

INTRODUCTION

11

Regulars and neighbors started filling up the room with friendly faces from open to close. The fastidious French artist who lived upstairs was eating three meals a day at the restaurant, joined by her loft neighbor, a clean-cut Swiss single father and his five-year-old daughter drawing on the placemats. A handsome gray-haired man who Maya had introduced herself to on the street (months prior while collecting signatures for the community board) came to spend hours drinking rosé outside with his boyfriend, their Cavalier King Charles Spaniel waiting patiently by their feet. Here was the It Girl/DJ/clothing designer poring over e-mails while eating her grapefruit and yogurt. Installed at a corner table, sipping cappuccinos, a cane balanced on her lap, is the lady who taught art classes for the past three decades in the basement of the building next door. The brawny gym owners from around the corner ordered protein-heavy feasts of steak and whole branzino at 11:00 P.M. The dapper maître d' from up the street came to the bar to chat with Maya while drinking a Negroni. They also befriended local artists who, in exchange for meals, donated artwork to fill the walls. The spirit of Freda traded in her twinkling costume jewelry and Elizabeth Taylor–esque bouffant for the likes of renowned painters in the downtown art scene, a graffiti artist, line drawings from a New Yorker cartoonist, and even one of Jack's Wife Freda's own waiters.

Within a year of opening, the restaurant was packed at any time of day. Maya and Dean had filled a niche in the neighborhood, a catchall of the true diversity of its streets; a comfortable, affordable, and congenial place where the food was unpretentious and the service was easy. That little café could hardly contain the following it garnered, so on its second anniversary they started to look for a second location. In December 2014, Jack's Wife Freda had a twin sister at 50 Carmine Street in the West Village.

Today, a 7:00 A.M. staff meeting, scheduled ninety minutes before breakfast service begins, is the only quiet moment in the SoHo restaurant. "Hellos and good-byes are who we are," Maya tells the servers for the hundredth time, as the puffy-eyed team sips coffee and nibbles quietly on the bagels and lox that Dean picked up the night before from Russ & Daughters. Some of the servers closed down the restaurant six hours earlier, while others are dressed in their striped-shirt uniforms with an eight-hour shift ahead of them. Remarkably, no one is cranky despite the early hour. "The door is an absolute priority for all of us," adds Dean, picking up Maya's sentence. "As always, we must remember to nurture our regulars and embrace the newbies. No one should ever come in here and feel we're too busy for them. Be loose, confident, and generous in spirit." Maya takes over for him, "And you guys know the drill: make sure the art is hanging straight and please keep an eye on things that need dusting." The meeting continues like this for an hour, the owners reiterating the mantras of their successful formula. Julia describes a new dish they're trying out on the menu called Maya's Grain Bowl. The staff asks questions and discusses how best to handle the incident earlier in the week of a disgruntled neighbor, who pointedly rammed her bicycle into the crowd of people on the sidewalk waiting for brunch tables.

Outside, a tourist family of four peeks through the windows. Maya immediately gestures for them to come inside. They open the door halfway and shyly ask if they've come too early. "Hi! No, come on in!" exclaims Maya, as if ushering friends into her home. "We're just finishing up our meeting, and the kitchen opens in thirty minutes. But sit—have some coffee! We also have bagels in the meantime." Dean turns to the staff and recites a credo that applies as much to the servers' shifts as it does to their philosophy of accommodation: "Remember: Early is on time." And with that, the meeting is over. The staff disperses, some lingering to chat for a bit. The servers tie on their aprons, begin setting up the dining room, and fix tea for the first table of the day. As Dean and Maya head out to go to Carmine Street, the tourist family flags them over. "Please tell Jack and Freda that we say thank you for our breakfast!" "Of course," they smile. The whole story is too long to tell in passing, but it is still deeply understood.

—Sarah Tihany

COOKING FROM THE
JACK'S WIFE FREDA MENU
AT HOME

Chef Julia Jaksic

When most of us think back to the nourishing food we were fed in our grandmas' kitchen, there is a sense of curative simplicity. The menu at Jack's Wife Freda was created to evoke that same ubiquitous comfort, while being versatile enough to order from multiple times a week—or even more than once in a day!

My desire to become a chef stems from my own grandmother, who immigrated from Croatia. She was, for all intents and purposes, a professional cook—feeding a family of five three times a day. Nana's recipes were usually complex in technique, yet they always tasted straightforward and delicious. One of her specialties was apple strudel. I have memories of her stretching the dough paper-thin over a tablecloth, without tearing even the tiniest of holes. At that point I was given free rein to run around the sides of the table with scissors, trimming the edges. Then Nana would roll up the filling of apples, sugar, and bread crumbs between what seemed like hundreds of layers of the delicate dough.

Over the years I've tried to reproduce her strudel but inevitably fall short. Though the recipe and ingredients are basic, they require a well-trained hand and the intangible qualities of grandmotherly love. I may never be able to perfect her pastries, but I continue to be inspired by her use of ingredients, technique, and her passion for good food prepared with fresh, nourishing ingredients. At Jack's Wife Freda, we have married classic bistro and café fare from around the world with the secrets we've borrowed from our grandmothers' recipe boxes.

As you turn these pages, you'll discover what a day at Jack's Wife Freda looks like for us—from the front of the house to the kitchens, with glimpses through the eyes of our guests and local regulars—and if you haven't paid a visit to the restaurants yet, please do stop by the next time you're in the neighborhood. But I also hope, as you bring these recipes into your own kitchen, that these dishes inspire the same spirit of community, conviviality, and love, and bring back one or two memories of the first foods that defined home and family for you. It's how Grandma Freda would have wanted it!

PANTRY AND COOKING BASICS

The recipes you will find in this book are very approachable for a home cook because the home kitchen is where they originated. The key to all these recipes is quality ingredients, so we suggest, when possible, using locally grown produce and dairy from your farmer's market.

One item we use exclusively from the farmer's market is eggs. They're always best from free-range chickens and you'll find that the more diverse the hen's diet is, the more beautiful the yolks will be to see and to taste.

Overall, the grain of kosher salt is most suitable for cooking, as it allows you to control the level of salinity in a dish. Kosher salt is commonly found in grocery stores.

There are a few products called for in this book that may require a specialty store:

ORANGE BLOSSOM WATER AND ROSE WATER.
These Middle Eastern staples are generally sold in the international section of many grocery stores, but if you are having trouble finding them, you can easily order them online.

LEBANESE YOGURT OR LABNEH.
This "yogurt" is actually a very thick and tart soft cheese. Again, it may only be available in specialty shops. A useful substitution in this case would be whole-milk Greek yogurt.

FRESH HERBS.
We love cooking with fresh herbs, as you will see throughout this book. Though you can easily find them in supermarkets, if you live in a space that allows you to grow herbs, there is nothing as satisfying as going out into your own garden and clipping them straight from the plant!

ZA'ATAR.
This all-purpose spice blend is used in many different kinds of Middle Eastern cooking. It's sprinkled onto breads, generously added to finish hummus, and liberally added to vegetables or fish. It's usually available in specialty shops or online as a premixed seasoning, but can easily be made at home. Simply combine equal parts white sesame seeds, dried thyme, dried oregano, and sumac.

There are a couple of tools that are essential in our kitchen and come in handy when cooking the recipes in this book:

MICROPLANE.

This versatile tool, primarily intended for zesting citrus, is also perfect for grating nutmeg, finely shaving a clove of garlic, or creating a pillowy blanket of Parmesan.

JAPANESE MANDOLINE.

This is an inexpensive alternative to its bulky French cousin. Always pay close attention while using a mandoline, as it can be deceptively sharp. The Japanese mandoline is plastic but still heavy-duty. Use it to grate beets for a grain bowl, shred carrots, and create thin slices of radish for garnishing.

Finally, here are a handful of recipes that we use in the restaurant for a wide variety of dishes and accompaniments. You may find them so delicious and popular that you'll want to keep a batch on hand for whenever the impulse strikes.

GARLIC BUTTER

Yields roughly ½ cup

6 garlic cloves

1 tablespoon packed flat-leaf parsley leaves

Pinch of kosher salt

8 tablespoons (1 stick) unsalted butter, at room temperature

Mince the garlic and finely chop the parsley leaves. Mix the garlic, parsley, and salt into the butter until very well combined. This will keep, refrigerated, for up to 2 weeks.

HOMEMADE MAYONNAISE

Yields roughly ½ cup

This flavorsome, versatile recipe can be used in any dish that calls for the store-bought equivalent.

1 small garlic clove

1 egg yolk

2 teaspoons fresh lemon juice

½ teaspoon Dijon mustard

¼ cup sunflower seed oil

¼ cup olive oil

Kosher salt

Finely grate the garlic clove with a Microplane into a small bowl with the egg yolk, lemon juice, and mustard. Whisk until fully combined.

Combine the sunflower seed and olive oils in a spouted measuring cup. In a very slow and steady stream, while whisking continuously, add the oils to the yolk mixture. The mixture will emulsify and become quite thick. Season with salt.

HOT SAUCE

Yields 1 cup

Maya and Dean both grew up being served spicy condiments (harissa in Israel and peri peri in South Africa, respectively) alongside the home-cooked meals from their grandmothers' kitchens. At Jack's Wife Freda we love the option of adding a spicy kick to any of our dishes. Our hot sauce goes with almost every item on our menu: from the steak and eggs at breakfast to the peri peri chicken at dinner. Many of our guests *insist* on dipping their French fries in it too. Don't be shy!

1 jalapeño chili

1 serrano chili

Optional: 1 habanero chili for extra heat

3 garlic cloves

2 bunches of cilantro, stems removed

¼ cup sunflower seed oil

Kosher salt

Slice the jalapeño and serrano chilies into ¼- or ½-inch rings, including the seeds. (For an extra-spicy hot sauce slice and add the habanero.)

Put the chilies into a blender with the garlic cloves and cilantro.

Add ¼ cup water and the oil and blend on high speed for 1 to 2 minutes, or until the mixture is smooth and consistent. Season with salt and additional water if the mixture is too thick.

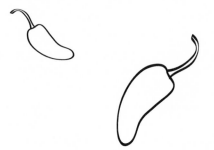

PERI PERI SPICE

Yields ¾ cup

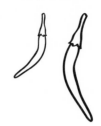

Nothing brings Dean back to his childhood in Johannesburg quite like the flavor of peri peri spice. The bird's-eye chili, though native to South America, was spread around the globe as a result of Spanish and Portuguese colonization. As these flavors trickled over the border from Mozambique, they wove their way into regional South African cuisine where they can be found today in virtually every kitchen, restaurant, and street cart. At Jack's Wife Freda, you can find our own spicy, smoky, slightly sweet version in our signature peri peri chicken dish, as a dry rub on our chicken kebabs, and as a gravy for our sweetbreads. Since it is difficult to find the African bird's-eye chili, we use the more commonly available árbol chili.

1 tablespoon ground árbol chili

5 tablespoons Hungarian paprika

3 tablespoons light brown sugar

1 tablespoon kosher salt

1 teaspoon ground cumin

½ teaspoon ground allspice

Pinch of ground cloves

Combine all the ingredients in a small bowl, mixing well so that the brown sugar is evenly distributed.

SALSA VERDE

Yields roughly 1 cup

This is an all-purpose sauce that can finish many dishes with a savory acidity. We serve it with poached eggs, chicken kebabs, and fish for a flavorful, tangy kick. It will last for 2 days, refrigerated, but is sure to vanish quickly once you've tried it.

1 cup packed flat-leaf parsley leaves

1 shallot

1 garlic clove

Zest of 1 lemon

1 tablespoon sherry vinegar

1 cup olive oil

Kosher salt

Chop the parsley very finely and transfer to a small bowl.

Finely mince the shallot and garlic, then add to the parsley.

Add the lemon zest to the parsley with the sherry vinegar.

Mix well by hand while slowly adding the olive oil.

Season with salt.

SMOKED PAPRIKA AIOLI

Yields roughly ½ cup

1 cup mayonnaise (for homemade, see page 18)

2 teaspoons smoked paprika

Zest of ½ lemon

In a large bowl, mix all the ingredients together. Use a rubber spatula to remove any lumps of paprika, stirring until uniform in color.

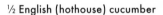

TZATZIKI

Yields 1½ cups

This classic Greek recipe is a condiment for some, a dip for others, and a favorite accompaniment for many dishes in Israel. We use a Lebanese yogurt called *labneh* to give the tzatziki its thicker consistency and tangier taste, but you can absolutely substitute strained Greek yogurt.

½ English (hothouse) cucumber

1 garlic clove

2 tablespoons fresh dill, stems removed

1 cup labneh or Greek yogurt

1 teaspoon red wine vinegar

1 teaspoon fresh lemon juice

1 tablespoon olive oil

Kosher salt

Using the largest holes on a box grater, shred the cucumber (including its skin).

Finely grate the garlic with a Microplane and coarsely chop the dill tops.

In a small bowl, combine the yogurt, shredded cucumber, garlic, red wine vinegar, lemon juice, olive oil, and dill. Stir to combine. Season with salt.

POACHED EGGS WITH ROASTED TOMATO AND HALOUMI

Yields 4 servings

This protein-packed dish is one of our favorite breakfasts! Haloumi is a slightly salty, savory cheese made from goat's or sheep's milk. It is super flavorful—imagine a marriage between feta and mozzarella—and makes for a great vegetarian alternative to ham or sausage. Don't be too concerned about using in-season tomatoes, because their flavors will concentrate as they cook in the oven. The tomatoes can also be made ahead of time and reheated.

4 plum tomatoes

2 tablespoons olive oil

Kosher salt

5 thyme sprigs, stems removed

1 (8-ounce) package haloumi cheese

4 Poached Eggs (page 33)

¼ cup Salsa Verde (page 19)

Preheat the oven to 375°F.

Wash the plum tomatoes and cut in half lengthwise.

Arrange the tomatoes, cut side up, on a baking rack over a baking sheet to catch any juices.

Drizzle the tomatoes with 1 tablespoon olive oil and season with salt. Finish by picking fresh thyme leaves, spreading them over all the tomatoes.

Bake for 1 hour and 15 minutes, or until the edges of the tomatoes begin to caramelize.

Cut the haloumi crosswise into ½-inch-thick slices.

Heat remaining 1 tablespoon olive oil over (or a little less if your pan is nonstick) in a cast-iron pan over high heat until very hot.

Sear the cheese until golden in color on both sides, 30 seconds to 1 minute per side, and transfer to a plate.

For each serving, begin by placing 2 oven-roasted tomatoes side by side on a plate. Place a slice of seared haloumi on each tomato, followed by a poached egg. Spoon a tablespoon of the salsa verde onto each egg, being sure to give the salsa a quick mix if need be before ladling it onto the egg.

We serve a slice of sourdough, toasted with a little olive oil, alongside this dish at Jack's Wife Freda, but any version of your favorite bread will do.

EGGS BENNY

Yields 4 servings

Eggs Benedict is the quintessential weekend brunch dish, but we put a colorful (and unconventional "Jewish delicatessen") twist on them. The fuchsia pink of the Beet Hollandaise makes us smile every time one goes out of the kitchen! It's best to use a cast-iron pan for making the latkes—a delicious alternative to potatoes or hash browns. You can cook these latkes for the Jewish holidays or special occasions, but we think they're great just about any time of the year.

6 parsley sprigs

8 Potato Latkes (see below)

8 ounces smoked salmon, sliced

8 Poached Eggs (page 33)

¾ cup Beet Hollandaise (recipe follows)

Pick the parsley leaves from their stems and coarsely chop them. Place 2 latkes on each plate and drape one piece of smoked salmon on top of each latke. Follow with one poached egg on top of each latke. Spoon 1 to 2 tablespoons of the hollandaise onto each. Finish with a sprinkling of the chopped parsley.

POTATO LATKES

Yields eight 3-inch latkes

1 shallot

1 teaspoon fresh thyme leaves

3 russet potatoes

2 large eggs

1½ teaspoons kosher salt, plus more as needed

¼ cup matzo meal

½ cup olive oil

Peel and mince the shallot; set aside. Finely chop the thyme leaves.

Peel the potatoes, covering each potato in cold water while you peel the next. Using the largest holes on a box grater, grate the peeled potatoes. Rinse the grated potatoes under cold water until the water runs clear, and gently squeeze out any excess water. Dry the potatoes lightly with a towel and place in a medium bowl.

In a separate bowl, whisk the eggs well. Add the shallot, thyme, and salt to the egg mixture and whisk to combine.

Add the eggs to the grated potatoes and stir well so that the potatoes are completely coated. Sprinkle the matzo meal onto the potatoes and once again stir to combine.

Heat a cast-iron pan over medium heat and add the olive oil. Using a tablespoon, form a heaping spoonful of potato mixture into discs by pressing it between your palms, taking care not to make the discs too thin. Cook on one side until golden brown, then flip and cook until the second side is golden brown, 3 to 4 minutes per side. Be diligent about keeping your heat at medium to medium-low. If the outside of your latke browns too quickly, the middle may still be raw! If this happens, just throw them into a 325°F oven for 5 to 10 minutes. Transfer to a plate and season with salt.

BEET HOLLANDAISE

Yields approximately ¾ cup

8 tablespoons (1 stick) unsalted butter

4 large egg yolks

1 tablespoon lemon juice

2 tablespoons beet juice or beet concentrate

Kosher salt

Place a small saucepan, filled halfway with water, over medium heat and bring the water to a simmer, then turn the heat to the lowest flame.

Melt the butter in a microwave or on the stovetop and transfer to a vessel that you can easily pour from.

In a metal or glass bowl that fits snugly on top of the pot of simmering water to create a double boiler, whisk the egg yolks, lemon juice, and beet juice. Place the bowl over the simmering water and whisk continuously until the egg mixture begins to thicken slightly. Add the butter in a slow, steady stream, whisking continuously. Remove from the heat and season with salt.

HOW TO
POACH EGGS

Yield varies

Poached eggs feature heavily on the breakfast menu at Jack's Wife Freda, but they make a wonderful simple meal any time of day and a great addition to salads as well as our grain bowl served at lunch.

1 Fill a saucepan three-quarters of the way with water and add a tablespoon of white wine vinegar and a pinch of kosher salt.

Bring the water to a simmer.

2 Crack an egg into a small bowl.

3 Swirl the water with a spoon.

4 Carefully add the egg to the water.

5 Let the egg simmer in the water for 2 to 3 minutes.

6 Carefully scoop out the egg with a slotted spoon.

POTATO LATKES WITH APPLE-CINNAMON YOGURT

Yields roughly 1 cup

When Jack was growing up in a small shtetl in Lithuania, his family sold latkes out of their home kitchen. His mother would fry up the hot, crispy pancakes, considered the best in town, while Jack and his siblings ran the shop and peeled an endless supply of potatoes. As an adult, he was always brought back to his childhood while whipping up a batch of these for his grandkids in South Africa.

Feel free to play around with the size of these latkes—we think smaller bite-size ones are perfect for dipping and snacking. While the apple-cinnamon yogurt can be prepared ahead of time, it is undoubtedly best served with a fresh, hot batch of latkes.

1 Granny Smith apple

1 teaspoon butter

¼ cup sugar

½ teaspoon ground cinnamon

8 ounces labneh or Greek yogurt

Potato Latkes (page 31)

Peel and core the apple and cut it into a small dice.

Melt the butter in a small sauté pan on medium-low heat and add the apple. Cook for 3 to 5 minutes, or until the apple just begins to soften, then add the sugar and cinnamon. Cooking for another 2 to 3 minutes, or until the apple lets out a little juice. Remove from the heat and allow to cool.

Gently fold the apple mixture into the yogurt and refrigerate for at least an hour.

Serve with potato latkes.

HOW TO
SOFT-BOIL EGGS

Yield varies

WHAT YOU'LL NEED

Free-Range Eggs

Saucepan

STEPS

Place the eggs in a saucepan. Add cold water to cover them by 1 inch.

(1)

Heat the water over high heat just until boiling. Turn off heat, cover, and leave for desired yolk texture. (See below.)

(2)

Once done, lift the eggs out of the pan with a slotted spoon. Place each into an egg cup.

(3)

TIMING THE YOLK

4 MINUTES
very runny

7 MINUTES
medium runny

9 MINUTES
almost firm

12 MINUTES
totally firm

JULIA'S GRANOLA

Yields about 4 cups/12 servings

Though we serve this nutty granola with grapefruit at Jack's Wife Freda, don't hesitate to add it to your favorite seasonal fruit, berries, yogurt, or almond milk for a light yet filling start to the day. Granola will keep for about 2 weeks in an airtight container.

½ cup raw almonds

½ cup Brazil nuts

3 cups rolled oats

¼ cup organic dark brown or muscovado sugar

⅓ cup maple syrup

⅓ cup sunflower seed oil

¼ teaspoon kosher salt

Preheat the oven to 250°F.

Coarsely chop the almonds and Brazil nuts. Mix the oats, chopped nuts, and brown sugar in a large bowl.

In a small bowl, whisk together the maple syrup, sunflower oil, and salt. Add the wet ingredients to the dry and mix well, until the oats are evenly coated.

Spread the mixture in an even layer on a baking sheet and bake for 1 hour, or until nicely golden, mixing once halfway through the baking process.

GRAPEFRUIT YOGURT

Yields 3 servings

Ruby red grapefruit has a wonderful natural sweetness. We love the way it pairs with the tartness of a thick yogurt and our crunchy granola. A drizzle of fragrant local honey is a sensational way to bring this dish together.

1 large or 2 small ruby red grapefruit

1½ cups labneh or Greek yogurt

¾ cup Julia's Granola (recipe above)

3 tablespoons honey

1 mint sprig

To supreme your grapefruit (or any citrus): Begin by cutting ½ inch off the top and bottom of the grapefruit. Standing the grapefruit securely on a cutting board, use your knife to follow the natural outer curve of the fruit, removing only the outer skin and white pith and as little of the flesh as possible. Once the fruit is skinned, notice the natural segments and cut along the inside of the membranes in a V shape. You will end up with segments of grapefruit without any membrane.

Divide the grapefruit among three small bowls. Scoop 2 heaping tablespoons (roughly ½ cup) of labneh into the bowls next to the grapefruit. Add ¼ cup of the granola between the yogurt and fruit. Drizzle honey over everything. Finish by placing a few mint leaves on top of each other, rolling them up, and thinly slicing them crosswise into thin strips. Garnish each bowl with a little mint.

BE PRESENT
HUG MORE
DUDE, SWEET.
SUGAR PIE HONEY
JACK
HUG MORE
HUG MORE
Y SWEET
DUDE, SWEET.
HUG MORE
SUGAR PIE
JACK
REDA

A DAY AT JACK'S WIFE FREDA

We open at 8:30 A.M. but people always come in a little early. Often they'll stand on the curb in hesitation, waiting for someone to beckon them in. Jack's Wife Freda is not the type of place to keep the door locked until we "open." If the chairs are off the tables and there is a place to sit while the coffee brews and the servers set up, then anyone is welcome. The first rush of the day: breakfast meetings and locals in for a familiar bite and not a few guests with damp hair and gym bags in tow. The restaurant is often full before we even receive all our daily deliveries. Pallets of dairy, meat, and vegetables slide through the open trap door.

There is a certain stamina required to get through an eight-hour shift but the energy from this early crowd propels our staff into the afternoon rush, which quiets again around 3:00 P.M. My job is to watch the entire room, from greeting people at the door to checking in on the kitchen to guiding the servers. "The Big Picture" is what we call it. If someone's soft-boiled eggs look overdone, or a guest looks a little confused when their meal is laid on the table, we want to make sure everyone is satisfied. Some people know exactly how to get what they want in a restaurant but most are apprehensive. Not only do we want people to get exactly what they had in mind, but every conversation opens the door for a new connection. There will always be mistakes, but they are also an opportunity to make a new friend and a regular.

In the height of the rush I wave to the newest couple at the door. Ten minutes, I tell them, and ask them to stay close. They stand on the curb next to the guy who cuts my hair and the couple who asked Dean to officiate their wedding. There's an ornery older man who heads right toward his favorite spot at the bar. During his first visit a server spilled hot sauce on his coat and he lost his temper. When Maya called him to apologize and offer to pay his dry-cleaning, he explained it was his first Christmas post-divorce without his children and apologized for his outburst. Now he comes in three or four times a week and shows me photos of his son's latest artwork. There's a woman getting up whose burger was undercooked; I thank her again for her patience and give her a fresh watermelon juice on her way out the door. The bartender shouts a thank-you from behind the espresso machine.

As the morning shift wraps up, the night crew begins to arrive. This is the most important time of the day. There are two teams of servers in striped shirts, one

easing into the end of a busy day and the other walking into a restaurant moving at full speed. Like relay runners, we hand off the care of all the guests and find a seat at our communal table. Everyone takes a breath, and then orders their favorite dish for a staff meal, sometimes a variation or secret compilation of menu items, perhaps accompanied by a glass of rosé. Within minutes, they are also part of the crowd, laughing over the music and sharing their latest personal successes in music, art, acting, or life.

—Patrick Hessert

DUCK BACON

Yields 4 servings

At Jack's Wife Freda we looked for an interesting alternative to bacon, careful not to deprive our customers of a smoky, salty breakfast option. This duck bacon is the result! Duck breasts have a top layer of fat, mimicking the indulgent crispiness of pork belly. Even if you love the pork version, this is a delicious substitute when you're up for something a little different. The smoking is the trickiest part of the process, though many kitchen stores sell small household smokers that work wonderfully for this. If you are lucky enough to have an outdoor smoker, that is certainly ideal.

¼ cup kosher salt

1 teaspoon pink pickling salt

¼ cup light brown sugar

4 thyme sprigs

1 bay leaf

½ teaspoon whole black peppercorns

2 duck breasts

2 ounces applewood chips, for smoking

In a small bowl, combine the salts, sugar, herbs, and spices; mix thoroughly.

Massage the salt mixture into the breasts, making sure to cover them completely. Put the breasts in a zip-top bag, seal, and refrigerate for 12 hours, turning the bag every few hours. As the breasts sit in the cure they will begin to firm slightly. After 12 hours, rinse the breasts and dry well.

Smoke the breasts using your smoker's specifications for 1 hour. Once finished, remove and chill.

Slice the duck breasts lengthwise into thin strips. Cook the duck bacon similarly to how you'd cook the pork version, which tastes best browned on each side for a few minutes over medium to high heat in a cast-iron pan.

HOW TO
MAKE YOUR OWN DUCK BACON

Yield varies

STEP 1

Trim duck breasts of any excess skin,
rinse under cold water, and dry slightly.

STEP 2

Mix salts, sugar, peppercorns, and
herbs.

STEP 3

Completely coat each duck breast with salt
mixture, taking care to press into all crevices.
Place in refrigerator in a plastic ziplock bag
or in a baking dish for 12 hours, turning meat
once or twice.

STEP 4

Rinse the duck under cold water and dry
thoroughly with paper towels.

STEP 5
Using your smoker, light the applewood chips and allow them to burn down.

STEP 6
Allow duck to smoke for 1 hour, remove from the smoker, and place in refrigerator.

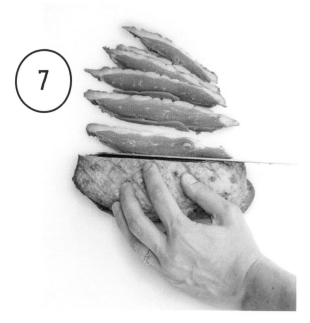

STEP 7
Once chilled, slice the duck lengthwise into long, thin strips.

STEP 8
Using a frying pan or cast-iron pan on a medium heat, brown each side of the bacon to your preference.

STEP 9:
ENJOY WITH EGGS, ON A MADAME FREDA (PAGE 51) OR A BLT, ETC.

MADAME FREDA

Yields 4 sandwiches

Oh, the pleasures of lingering over a croque madame in a Parisian café! This decadent sandwich is borrowed from the wonderful French version, and we've substituted our delicious—and addictive—duck bacon for the classic ham. This makes a great brunch dish and we recommend using high-quality cheese for the tastiest results. The béchamel should be made ahead of time so that it can chill for at least an hour.

BÉCHAMEL

½ cup whole milk

½ cup heavy cream

Pinch of kosher salt

2 tablespoons butter

2 tablespoons flour

1 teaspoon Worcestershire sauce

½ cup shredded white cheddar cheese

8 slices sourdough or country white bread

8 slices Gruyère or Swiss cheese

8 slices Duck Bacon (page 47), cooked

Butter, for toasting

½ cup white cheddar cheese

½ cup shredded Parmesan cheese

4 eggs

Cracked black pepper

For the béchamel: Heat the milk, cream, and salt together in a microwave or in a saucepan on the stovetop until warm. Slowly melt the butter in a saucepan, and once melted, add the flour and stir until combined. Slowly whisk in the warm milk and cream and bring the béchamel to a simmer. Once thickened and bubbling, add the Worcestershire sauce and ½ cup of the cheddar cheese; stir to combine. Chill in the refrigerator.

To assemble the sandwiches: Preheat the broiler.

Spread a teaspoon or so of the béchamel on both sides of the bread slices. Place 2 slices of Gruyère and 2 slices of duck bacon on one side of the sandwich. Close the sandwich and do the same for the other three.

In a frying pan, using a small amount of butter, toast each side of the sandwich as you would a grilled cheese.

Mix together the cheddar and the Parmesan in a small bowl. Place the toasted sandwiches on a baking sheet and spread liberally with the béchamel covering the entire slice, doing the same with a handful of the shredded cheese. Place the baking sheet under your broiler and cook for 2 to 4 minutes, until the top of the sandwich is bubbling and the cheese becomes a golden brown.

In a small sauté pan, cook each egg sunny-side up with a little butter; the yolks should stay runny. Place one egg on top of each sandwich. Serve with a dash of Worcestershire sauce and cracked black pepper.

ORANGE BLOSSOM PANCAKES

Yields 8 to 10 pancakes

Oranges are synonymous with breakfast, and at Jack's Wife Freda we use the fragrant water from the orange blossom for a slightly Middle Eastern nod to the classic pancake. You can find orange blossom water in Middle Eastern specialty stores or very easily online. Serve these with labneh and Honey Syrup—orange or citrus marmalade makes a tart and delightful addition, too.

2 cups flour

2½ teaspoons baking powder

½ teaspoon baking soda

¼ teaspoon kosher salt

2 tablespoons sugar

2 large eggs

2 cups buttermilk

3 tablespoons orange blossom water

Labneh and orange marmalade, for serving

Honey Syrup (recipe follows), for serving

In a large bowl, whisk together the flour, baking powder, baking soda, salt, and sugar. In a smaller bowl, whisk together the eggs, buttermilk, and orange blossom water. Stir the egg mixture into the flour mixture until just combined, being very careful not to overmix.

Heat a greased griddle over medium heat. Ladle the batter into pancakes of roughly 4 inches in diameter. Once they begin to puff and small bubbles appear on the surface, it's time to flip. Both sides should be golden brown.

To serve, spoon on a generous amount of labneh and orange marmalade (we love to use the typical British style) on top. Serve with Honey Syrup!

HONEY SYRUP

Yields 2 cups

In lieu of maple syrup we make our own sweet honey syrup to serve with waffles and pancakes. Feel free to experiment: Using different types of honey will alter the flavors and bring out the varied aromas of the bees' harvest. Honey Syrup can be stored for up to a month, refrigerated, in an airtight container.

1 orange, or 2 pieces of orange zest

1 cup honey of your choice

1 teaspoon pure vanilla extract, or ½ fresh vanilla bean

Using a peeler, hold the orange securely and peel the zest from top to bottom. Combine all the ingredients with ¾ cup water in a small saucepan over high heat. Stir continually until the syrup just comes to a boil, turn off the heat, and let the syrup cool. You can discard the orange peel (and vanilla bean, if you used one) once the mixture is cooled.

ROSE WATER WAFFLES

Yields 6 to 8 waffles

Rose water is a delicate flavor used in many Middle Eastern pastries. We added it to these waffles because the nuttiness of the brown butter and the subtle floral note of the rose water brought out a perfect marriage of flavors. It's easy to find rose water in most grocery stores or online. These are delicious topped with our Honey Syrup, a dollop of labneh or Greek yogurt, a handful of fresh berries, or your favorite waffle accompaniment.

2½ cups flour

2 teaspoons baking powder

½ teaspoon baking soda

½ teaspoon kosher salt

1 tablespoon sugar

3 large eggs

1¼ cups whole milk

2 tablespoons rose water

1 cup sour cream

4 tablespoons (½ stick) unsalted butter

¼ cup honey

Fresh berries, for serving

Yogurt, for serving

Honey Syrup (page 53), for serving

Mix the flour, baking powder, baking soda, salt, and sugar in a large bowl to combine.

In a separate bowl, whisk together the eggs, milk, rose water, and sour cream.

In a small sauté pan, melt the butter over medium heat, swirling the pan until the butter begins to brown (be careful, as the butter may splatter). When the butter begins forming brown bits on the bottom of the pan and the color is a deep golden brown, turn off the heat. Scrape up any bits of burnt butter from the bottom of the pan and add the honey to the warm butter, stirring until smooth.

Add the egg mixture to the sifted dry ingredients and mix just until combined. Add the butter-honey mixture to the waffle batter and stir just to combine, taking care not to overmix.

Heat a waffle iron, spray each side with nonstick cooking spray, and cook the waffles until golden brown, or to your waffle iron specifications.

Finish with a topping of berries, a dollop of yogurt, and a pour of Honey Syrup.

HOT GRAIN BOWL

Yields 6 to 8 servings

There is nothing like a hot bowl of porridge on a cold winter morning. This recipe is a great alternative to oatmeal and can be loaded with your favorite fruits, nuts, and seeds—anything goes! Quinoa is a good source of vegetable protein, which makes this dish a great start to the day. We keep this recipe dairy-free, but any type of milk is fine. Other flavor combinations that work well are blueberries with slivered almonds and flaxseed, or pomegranate seeds with chopped pistachio and persimmon.

½ cup red quinoa

½ cup white quinoa

2 cups almond milk

1 cup coconut milk

¼ teaspoon salt

1 teaspoon ground cinnamon

¼ teaspoon ground cardamom

2 tablespoons honey

Toppings of your choice

Combine all the ingredients in a saucepan over medium-low heat. Stir every few minutes to prevent any of the quinoa from sticking to the bottom of the pan. Once the liquid has nearly all been absorbed and the quinoa is quite soft, 25 to 30 minutes (this may be longer than the instructions say on your package, so test once for texture), remove from the heat.

Ladle the quinoa into bowls and top with fresh fruit, nuts, seeds, or additional sweeteners. Any leftovers can be refrigerated and reheated by adding a little extra almond milk.

GREEN SHAKSHUKA

Yields 2 quarts sauce, roughly 8 to 10 servings

Shakshuka (*shahk-SHOO-ka*) is a dish of Tunisian origin, possibly dating back to the Ottoman Empire, and possessively beloved by Libyans, Egyptians, Moroccans, Algerians, and Israelis alike. Simply put, it's a traditional Middle Eastern breakfast and lunch dish consisting of baked eggs and tomatoes. Growing up in Israel, Maya tried many different incarnations—each family's variation subtly different and fiercely defended. We knew we wanted a shakshuka on our menu and it needed to be spectacular. This interpretation of the dish lends a more Latin American spin to the classic tomato sauce. We love the fresh zestiness of the tomatillos, the richness of the egg yolks, and the doughiness of the toasted challah. Ours may break with tradition, but we think that rolling the word "shakshuka" off your tongue is nearly as delicious as eating our version of it!

1 large Spanish onion

6 garlic cloves

2 tablespoons olive oil

1½ teaspoons kosher salt

1½ pounds tomatillos

1 green bell pepper

1 jalapeño chili

½ cup packed fresh cilantro leaves

1 teaspoon ground coriander

1 teaspoon ground cumin

1 to 3 tablespoons Hot Sauce (page 18), if you like it spicy!

1 to 2 eggs per person

Chopped fresh parsley, for garnish

Toasted challah or French brioche, for serving

Preheat the oven to 300°F.

Peel and quarter the onion and place with the garlic cloves in a small baking dish. Drizzle with the olive oil and ½ teaspoon of the salt. Cover with aluminum foil and bake for 30 minutes, or until very soft when pierced with a knife. (The onion and garlic can be prepared ahead of time.)

In a large bowl, soak the tomatillos in warm water to peel off the outer husk, then cut in half. Cut the stem from the bell pepper, discard the seeds, and cut into quarters. Also cut the stem from the jalapeño, discard the seeds, and quarter.

Place the peeled tomatillos, bell pepper, jalapeño, and cilantro leaves in a food processor with the roasted onion and garlic. Process until very smooth; it will have a salsa-like consistency.

Transfer to a medium saucepan. Add the coriander, cumin, and remaining 1 teaspoon salt. Bring to a simmer over medium-high heat and cook for 2 to 3 minutes, or until the tomatillo sauce is heated through. Be careful not to cook too long or your sauce will discolor and the taste will change. Add 1 tablespoon of hot sauce at a time until you've hit your desired spice level.

To assemble the shakshuka: Oil a cast-iron pan and set it over low heat. Crack the desired number of eggs into the pan and cover. Allow the eggs to cook sunny-side up until the whites are fully cooked but the yolks remain soft (you can of course cook the yolks through if that is your preference).

Once the eggs are cooked, liberally spoon the shakshuka sauce on top of the eggs and garnish with chopped parsley. Serve with toasted challah or French brioche.

WE MET AT JACK'S—KIND OF. IT'S A LONG STORY . . .

Dean and I go way back—years ago, I lived above Schiller's Liquor Bar on the Lower East Side, where he worked, and it was there that I was first introduced to his hospitality. I was more than happy to follow him when he left to open Jack's Wife Freda with Maya. Lafayette Street soon became the spot. I came for the food, but I stayed for the people, by far the most inviting, sincere restaurant staff in New York City. Jack's Wife feels like a community, with familiar faces and memorized menu favorites. I couldn't go a week without my Jack's breakfast (over-easy with a side of extra green sauce) and a Nana Tea.

I can't remember whether I was coming in the door or leaving the day that Dean told me about a "dream girl" he wanted to introduce me to. Dean and Maya are like family, so I was pretty intrigued when he proposed a matchmaking scenario. He sent me dream girl's contact via text . . . and the rest is history. Courtney and I have been together for almost three years and we're a perfect match. We've since moved to California, though we are fortunate enough to work bicoastal, and every time we're back in the city, our first stop is Jack's. We are forever grateful to Dean and Maya for bringing us together, and to be a part of the community. Now, when will Jack's Wife come to LA?! The West Coast needs some better cantaloupe juice.

—Luke Wessman

RINKS

NANA TEA

Yields 1 serving

Welcome to high tea, Moroccan-style. "Nana" simply translates to "mint" in Arabic—specifically, robust Moroccan spearmint—and this leaf is nature's perfect digestif. Serving Nana Tea is symbolic of warmth and hospitality in the Middle East, where Maya and Dean spent many afternoons lingering over mint teas and people watching from the sidewalk cafés of Tel Aviv. At Jack's Wife Freda we love serving this tea to our guests, encouraging them to take their time before or after a meal over some fresh Nana Tea.

1 black tea bag

4 mint sprigs

Honey

Steep the tea bag in 10 to 12 ounces boiling water for 2 minutes. Add the mint and honey to taste.

AVOCADO AND KALE SHAKE

Yields 1 serving

This is an easy, quick breakfast or perfect midday pick-me-up. Feel free to use your favorite milk. The color is fantastic!

1 cup firmly packed chopped kale leaves

1 ripe banana, frozen, sliced

¼ avocado

1½ cups almond milk (or nut milk of your choice)

Make sure the kale is cut into pieces that will blend easily in your blender or Vitamix. Place the banana, kale, avocado, and almond milk in a blender. Blend for at least a minute, or until the kale has been broken down and the color of the shake is a bright, leafy green.

JACK'S WIFE FREDA

JACK'S WIFE FREDA

CANTALOUPE JUICE

Yields approximately 4 cups or servings

Cantaloupe juice is such an unexpectedly refreshing drink, velvety and sweet. We serve most of our cold, nonalcoholic beverages in takeaway cups because they are the perfect thing to sip while strolling down the streets of New York. The key to this recipe is a very good, very ripe cantaloupe. Look for a cantaloupe that feels heavy for its size and leave it to ripen at room temperature for 2 or 3 days, until it develops a pleasantly floral and sweet smell. If your melon doesn't ripen perfectly, just add a touch of sweetener: honey, agave, date sugar, or organic granulated sugar.

1 whole ripe cantaloupe

Sweetener of choice

Using a large knife, cut off the top and bottom of the cantaloupe. Stand the melon on a flat surface and remove the outer rind, following the natural curve of the melon in a downward motion, taking care not to cut off the fruit. Once the cantaloupe is peeled, cut it in half and scoop out the seeds.

Coarsely chop the melon into small pieces and place in a blender starting with 1 cup water. Blend on the highest speed, gradually adding more water until the consistency is more of a juice than a smoothie. Add sweetener of your choice to taste. Refrigerate until cold. Serve by itself or over ice.

MINT LEMONADE

Yields 2 cups

A wonderful summer drink slightly sweetened by our mint syrup but still pleasantly sour from the fresh lemon juice, topped with seltzer water for an effervescent finish. Feel free to adjust the proportion of ingredients here to suit your taste—some prefer the emphasis on lemonade, others on the fizz.

MINT SYRUP

Yields roughly ½ cup

½ cup sugar

½ ounce fresh mint (10 to 15 sprigs), plus a sprig for garnish

MINT LEMONADE

2 tablespoons fresh lemon juice

1½ cups seltzer

In a small saucepan, combine the sugar, ½ cup water, and the mint. Bring to a boil, turn the heat to low, and allow to simmer for 5 minutes. Let cool. Remove and discard the mint leaves once the syrup has cooled.

In a tall glass, stir together the lemon juice and 2 tablespoons of the mint syrup. Fill the glass with ice cubes and pour the seltzer over. Stir well to combine; add the mint sprig to garnish. Leftover syrup can be refrigerated in an airtight container for up to 2 weeks.

PEA AND RICOTTA TOAST

Yields 4 servings

In the springtime when everything starts turning green, this is a beautiful dish to celebrate with! Fresh peas are best, dropped into boiling salted water for 2 minutes and then dunked in a quick ice-water bath before following the directions. If you're using frozen peas, just make sure to thaw them out first.

1 shallot

2 garlic cloves

1 tablespoon olive oil, plus extra for drizzling

2 cups fresh or frozen peas (see head note)

¼ cup fresh mint leaves

1 cup ricotta

Zest of ½ lemon

Kosher salt

4 radishes

2 cups pea tendrils, baby arugula, or watercress

Lemon juice

4 slices seeded bread

Peel the shallot and garlic and coarsely chop into a small dice. In a sauté pan over low heat, cook the shallot and garlic with 1 tablespoon olive oil until they are soft and translucent. Add the peas to the pan and turn the heat to medium. Cook until there is no residual water left from the peas.

In a food processor, combine the peas and mint leaves and process until smooth, scraping down the sides of the container at least once. Add the ricotta and lemon zest to the pea mixture and process until combined. Transfer the mixture to a bowl and season with salt. Refrigerate until cool.

In the meantime, thinly slice the radishes and toss them with the greens. Add lemon juice and olive oil to taste.

Toast the bread and heap each slice with an equal serving of the pea-ricotta spread. Garnish each with radish salad and drizzle with olive oil.

Prego Roll
Portuguese skirt steak sandwich with garlic butter

MATZO BALL SOUP

Yields 8 servings/8 matzo balls

The age-old matzo ball rivalry! As iconic as it was in your grandma's home, it's equal in status in New York City dining culture. Whether served in your corner Jewish deli or a Michelin-starred restaurant, arguments will ensue over whose matzo ball prevails in greatness. Freda worked her whole life trying to perfect the ball—a worthy battle for a timeless recipe. We threw our hat in the ring and chose to substitute the usual chicken fat (schmaltz) with duck fat, hopefully distinguishing ours just enough from all the beloved matzo balls out there! Duck fat can be purchased at specialty grocery stores, usually in the refrigerated section. If you have a hard time finding it, you can render the fat from one duck breast by scoring the skin and cooking the breast, fat side down, over very low heat. Make sure to strain the fat before using.

2 pounds chicken bones

2 small yellow onions

3 carrots plus 1 large carrot and sliced

2 celery stalks

1 bunch parsley

1 tablespoon whole black peppercorns

1 bay leaf

1 cup matzo meal

1½ teaspoons onion powder

1½ teaspoons garlic powder

1 tablespoon baking powder

½ teaspoon kosher salt

¼ cup duck fat

4 eggs

3 dill sprigs

Preheat the oven to 400°F.

Place the chicken bones on a baking sheet and roast for 45 minutes to 1 hour, turning the bones halfway through cooking. The bones should be a golden brown; if they are roasted too dark, your stock will be bitter. Transfer the roasted bones to a large stockpot.

Peel and halve the onions. Halve the whole carrots and celery stalks and place all the vegetables on the baking sheet the chicken bones were roasted on, coating the vegetables in any fat that may be left in the pan. Roast the vegetables for 15 minutes. Transfer the vegetables, discard any fat, and scrape any bits left on the bottom of the sheet pan, to the stockpot with the chicken bones and cover with enough water that all the bones and vegetables are submerged.

Using kitchen string, tightly tie the parsley stems together and cut the stems from the leafy tops. Add the tied parsley stems to the stock; reserve the parsley leaves for another purpose. Finally, add the black peppercorns and bay leaf to the stockpot. Bring to a boil, then turn down to a very low simmer and cook for 30 to 45 minutes, or until the stock has reduced by a quarter. Skim the top layer of fat from the stock while it cooks. Strain the stock into a clean stockpot and cool.

In a medium bowl, mix the matzo meal, onion powder, garlic powder, baking powder, and salt.

If you're using already-rendered duck fat, measure and melt it in a microwave for 30 seconds. Whisk the eggs until combined, add the duck fat, and whisk again.

Stir the wet ingredients into the dry ingredients and mix thoroughly until the mixture starts to thicken. Cover the matzo ball mix and refrigerate for 30 minutes.

recipe continues

Using a large spoon, scoop a heaping amount of matzo mix (about 1½ ounces), roll into a ball, and set onto a plate lined with wax paper. If the matzo balls stick to your hands, massage a little oil into your hands. You should end up with 8 matzo balls, roughly the same size. Refrigerate the matzo balls once more for 30 minutes.

Bring the chicken stock to a simmer, season with salt, and add the matzo balls. Cover the pot and cook for 20 minutes.

Put one matzo ball in each bowl, ladle the chicken stock over, and garnish with chopped dill and thinly sliced carrot.

AVOCADO TOAST

Yields 4 servings

Avocado toast has taken the world by storm. There are so many variations of this simple but mouth-watering staple. The go-to recipe for most calls for a combination of lemon, olive oil, and chili flakes, though in the spirit of reinterpretation Julia added her favorite tomato jam recipe and a quick pickled carrot to the mix to add zing to the creaminess of ripe avocados. Tomato jam makes a great accompaniment to baked fish or spread on a sandwich. The pickled carrots are a welcome addition to coleslaw or Maya's Grain Bowl (page 117).

TOMATO JAM

1 small shallot

1 garlic clove

1 tablespoon olive oil

1 pint (approximately 2 cups) cherry tomatoes, cut in half lengthwise

¼ teaspoon chili flakes

½ teaspoon kosher salt

⅛ teaspoon ground allspice

2 tablespoons brown sugar

2 tablespoons sherry vinegar

1 teaspoon lemon zest

CARROT SLAW

2 cups shredded carrots

2 thyme sprigs

¼ cup apple cider vinegar

1 teaspoon kosher salt

1 tablespoon brown sugar

2 ripe avocados

Juice of ½ lemon

Kosher salt

Four 1-inch-thick slices multigrain bread

1 tablespoon za'atar (page 16)

For the tomato jam: Peel and mince the shallot and garlic and set aside. In a small saucepan, heat the olive oil over high heat and add the cherry tomatoes. Cook for 2 to 3 minutes, or just until the tomatoes start to sizzle. Add the shallot, garlic, chili flakes, salt, and allspice, stirring to combine. Add the brown sugar and sherry vinegar and stir. Turn the heat down to medium and allow the liquid to cook into the tomatoes, stirring the tomatoes every few minutes. Once there is no liquid left, about 10 minutes, turn off the heat and add the zest to the tomato jam, stirring to combine. Transfer the jam to a container and let cool at room temperature.

For the carrot slaw: Put the carrots into a medium bowl with the thyme sprigs. Heat ¼ cup water, the vinegar, salt, and sugar together in a small saucepan over medium-low heat. Stir the pickling liquid until all the sugar and salt has dissolved. Pour over the carrots and let cool, mixing every few minutes. Once the liquid has cooled, drain the carrots and discard the liquid.

Cut the avocados in half, discard the seeds, and scoop the flesh into a small bowl. Add the lemon juice and season with salt. Mash the avocado with a fork and stir until the mixture is somewhat smooth. It's okay to leave a few chunks of avocado.

Toast the bread and spread each slice liberally with the mashed avocado. Add a sprinkling of za'atar to each, then top the toasts with carrot slaw and a dollop of tomato jam.

HOUSE SALAD

Yields 4 to 6 servings

This recipe is really a general outline for a delicious, light, and crisp salad. It is not always easy to find watermelon radishes, though more often than not your local greenmarket will carry them in spring and summer. They are beautiful and vibrant, with a spicy crunch. When they are not available you can substitute thinly sliced raw baby beets or turnips. The salad is just as good with any other type of thinly shaved crunchy vegetable too.

4 red radishes

1 watermelon radish

1 large carrot

2 heads Boston or Bibb lettuce

1 ripe avocado

Kosher salt

Tarragon Vinaigrette (recipe follows)

1 cup pea shoots, sunflower sprouts, or microgreens

On a mandoline or with a sharp knife, carefully slice the radishes and carrot into paper-thin slices. Transfer to a bowl of ice water and place in the refrigerator for at least 15 minutes or up to a day.

Cut the stems from the lettuces and arrange the leaves on a large serving platter, discarding any outer leaves that are discolored or torn.

Arrange the vegetable slices over the lettuce leaves. Peel and pit the avocado and cut it into small wedges. Scatter these on top of the lettuce and vegetables. Sprinkle a few pinches of kosher salt over the salad and spoon the tarragon vinaigrette liberally over everything. Finish with a garnish of sprouts or microgreens.

TARRAGON VINAIGRETTE

Yields about ⅔ cup

2 tablespoons white wine vinegar

1 teaspoon Dijon mustard

1 garlic clove, minced

½ cup olive oil

2 tablespoons finely chopped fresh tarragon

Kosher salt

Whisk the vinegar, mustard, and garlic in a small bowl until combined. In a slow, steady stream, begin adding the olive oil, whisking continuously until emulsified. Finish by whisking in the tarragon and season with salt.

SOUP

MA

Jack's Bu
grilled tomato

Prego Roll
Portuguese skirt steak sand

Chicken Prego
grilled chicken breast with smoked paprika aioli & wate

Eggplant Baguette
tomato, mozzarella, olive tapenade & pesto

14 —

11 —

Mint L

TRY OUR
HOT SAUCE!

SIDES $6

Arugula Salad

GREEK SALAD

Yields 4 to 6 servings

Forget the stereotype of kids not eating their greens! Maya and Dean both grew up in households where enormous fresh salads were a staple of their diets. The iconic Greek Salad was a favorite and they wanted to update the crisp, salty salad to be hearty enough to stand alone as a meal. In lieu of romaine, we use two types of kale as a textural base—and you can even toss in a Chicken Kebab (page 105) for a substantial lunch. If you cannot find an English cucumber, look for an alternative thin-skinned cucumber, such as a pickling or Persian variety. Our pickled red onions add a zippy note to this salad and make a great addition to sandwiches and burgers, too.

1 bunch curly kale

1 bunch Tuscan (lacinato) kale

Kosher salt

Red Wine Vinaigrette (recipe follows)

1 English (hothouse) cucumber

1 pint cherry tomatoes

½ cup pitted salt-cured black olives

½ cup Pickled Red Onions (recipe follows)

¼ pound feta cheese

Wash and dry the kale and cut out any large stems. Cut the kale into thin strips crosswise and put in a large bowl. Lightly salt the kale and dress with ¼ cup of red wine vinaigrette. Massage the vinaigrette into the kale, tossing gently with your hands.

Cut the cucumber into small, bite-size pieces. Cut the cherry tomatoes in half. Cut the olives in half.

Add the tomatoes, cucumber, pickled onions, and olives to the bowl over the kale. Drizzle an additional 2 tablespoons of vinaigrette over the vegetables and mix with the kale. Once mixed, taste to determine if you need extra vinaigrette or salt and add accordingly. Top with ¼-inch-thick slices of feta.

PICKLED RED ONIONS

Yields roughly ½ to 1 cup

1 large red onion

½ cup red wine vinegar

1 tablespoon sugar

2 teaspoons kosher salt

1 bay leaf

Peel the onion and cut into quarters. Remove the center few pieces of the onion, especially if they are green. Julienne the quarters lengthwise, roughly ⅛ inch thick, being careful not to cut too thin.

In a small saucepan, mix ½ cup water, the vinegar, sugar, and salt. Heat to just a boil, stirring to make sure the sugar and salt have dissolved. Add the bay leaf to the liquid and pour over the onions. Cover with plastic wrap and cool. Drain and discard any liquid before eating.

RED WINE VINAIGRETTE

Yields 1 cup

¼ cup red wine vinegar

1 tablespoon Dijon mustard

1 teaspoon sugar

¼ teaspoon kosher salt

¾ cup olive oil

1 teaspoon dried oregano

Kosher salt and black pepper

In a small bowl, combine the vinegar, mustard, sugar, and salt. In a slow, steady stream, begin adding the olive oil while whisking continuously. Finish by whisking in the dried oregano. If the dressing seems too thick, thin it out with a little water. Season with salt and pepper.

JACK'S WIFE FREDA
SIDES $6
SANDWICHES
SMOKED SALMON AND AVOCADO TOAST
FREDA'S MATZO BALL SOUP $8
ENTREES
GRILLED HALOUMI $10
SALADS
BREAKFAST

APRIKA EGG SALAD

Yields 2 to 3 sandwiches

Seek out a loaf of French brioche for this recipe—its subtle sweetness and buttery crumb complements the lemony zing of the egg salad. We make this as an open-faced sandwich, but of course you can go the traditional route, too.

4 eggs

8 to 10 fresh chives

2 tablespoons mayonnaise (see page 18)

blespoons Dijon mustard

aprika

paprika

Zest of 1 sma   lemon

2 tablespoons fresh lem   ice

Kosher s

ioche

watercress

1 tablespoon olive oil

In a medium saucepan, cover the eggs with water and bring the water to a boil, turn off the heat, and cover the pan. Let the eggs sit for 10 to 12 minutes, submerge in ice water, then peel and finely chop them, then put them into a medium bowl.

Using a very sharp knife, finely chop the chives. In a small bowl, combine the mayonnaise, Dijon mustard, paprikas, lemon zest 1 tablespoon and lemon juice, and of the zest and mix well. Add the chives and season with salt. Add the dressing to the chopped eggs and mix well.

Toast the brioche and heap egg salad on top of each slice. Garnish with a quick salad of watercress dressed with the remaining 1 tablespoon lemon juice and the olive oil.

MAYA'S GRAIN BOWL

Yields 2 grain bowls

This is by far one of our most popular lunch dishes! We change the ingredients seasonally depending on what fresh local vegetables are available. The recipe below is based on our winter grain bowl and brings much-needed color to the table in the dead of winter. There are many components to this dish, but don't be overwhelmed by all these steps! None require much prep time, and the end result should be served at room temperature, making it easy to prepare ahead of time and to pull everything together in the end. If the oil has separated from the sesame paste in your tahini, make sure to stir well before using.

2 eggs

2 sweet potatoes

6 tablespoons olive oil

1½ teaspoons honey

3 teaspoons kosher salt

1 small shallot

½ cup red quinoa

4 garlic cloves

2 cups (roughly 1 pound) Brussels sprouts

1 large or 2 small red beets

1 bay leaf

¼ cup white wine vinegar

⸱aspoons sugar

ɩ large head kale

¼ cup tahini

1 teaspoon ground turmeric

Pinch of cayenne

For the soft-boiled eggs: In a saucepan, cover the eggs with water and bring the water to a boil. Turn off the heat and cover for 6 minutes. Immediately submerge the eggs into ice water then peel.

For the sweet potatoes: Preheat the oven to 350°F. Wash the sweet potatoes and cut each in half. Cut each half into 6 to 8 wedges and place in a large bowl. Drizzle 1 tablespoon of the olive oil and the honey onto the potatoes and toss. Add ½ teaspoon of the salt and toss again so that all the potatoes are evenly coated. Roast the potatoes on a baking sheet for 15 minutes. Turn each piece of sweet potato and continue roasting for an additional 15 minutes. Pierce a few pieces of sweet potato with the tip of a small knife; it should pierce the potato very easily. However, if you find the potatoes are still not soft, roast for an additional 5 to 10 minutes. Transfer the sweet potatoes to a plate and allow to cool. Raise the oven temperature to 450°F.

For the red quinoa: Peel and mince the shallot. In a small saucepan over medium-low heat, heat 2 teaspoons of the olive oil and add the minced shallot. Sauté the shallot until soft and translucent, roughly 5 minutes. Rinse the quinoa under cold water and add to the pan. Add 1 cup water and 1 teaspoon of the salt, stir, and turn the heat up to high. Once the water begins to boil, lower the heat to maintain a simmer and cover the pot. Cook for roughly 15 minutes, or until all the water has evaporated. Leave the lid on for 5 minutes after cooking so the quinoa can steam. Set aside.

For the Brussels sprouts: Mince 2 garlic cloves and add to a large bowl with 1 tablespoon of the olive oil; stir to combine. Trim the bottoms from the Brussels sprouts and cut in half, discarding any leaves that fall off. Toss the sprouts in the bowl with the garlic and oil, making sure all of them have been coated evenly. Sprinkle in a few pinches of salt and toss once again. Transfer to a baking sheet and bake for 10 to 15 minutes, turning once or twice during roasting. They should be crisp on the outside but soft on the inside and easily pierced with a tip of a knife. Set aside.

For the beets: Peel the beets. Using either a mandoline or a food processor, shred them to a slawlike consistency and place in a small bowl with the bay leaf. Combine the vinegar, ¼ cup water, the sugar, and 1 teaspoon of the salt. Bring to a boil on the stovetop or in a microwave. Stir to make sure all the sugar and salt has dissolved. Pour the hot pickling liquid on top of the beets. Cover with plastic wrap, pressing the plastic wrap down directly on top of the beets and making sure all the beets are covered with liquid. Place in the refrigerator to cool.

For the kale: Wash the kale and shake the leaves to dry slightly. Cut across into 1-inch ribbons, removing the thick stems. Mince the remaining 2 garlic cloves. In a large sauté pan on low heat, heat 1 tablespoon of the olive oil and the minced garlic. Toast the garlic to a light golden color, then add the kale and 2 tablespoons water. Allow the kale to steam and wilt slightly, adding extra water if the pan is dry. Finish with a few pinches of salt. Set aside.

For the turmeric tahini dressing: In a blender, combine the tahini, ⅓ cup water, the turmeric, and the cayenne; blend until smooth. Add the remaining 2 tablespoons olive oil and season with salt. Some brands of tahini will cause this sauce to thicken differently. If yours is too thick, add an additional tablespoon of water to thin it out.

Choose a wide shallow bowl and think of plating each vegetable like slices of pizza: Begin by spooning red quinoa toward the center, out to the rim of the bowl, then follow with the sautéed kale, roasted brussels sprouts, then the sweet potatoes, and finish by connecting it all with the pickled beets. Cut your soft-boiled eggs in half and place in the middle. Serve with turmeric tahini dressing on the side.

HOW TO
BUILD A GRAIN BOWL

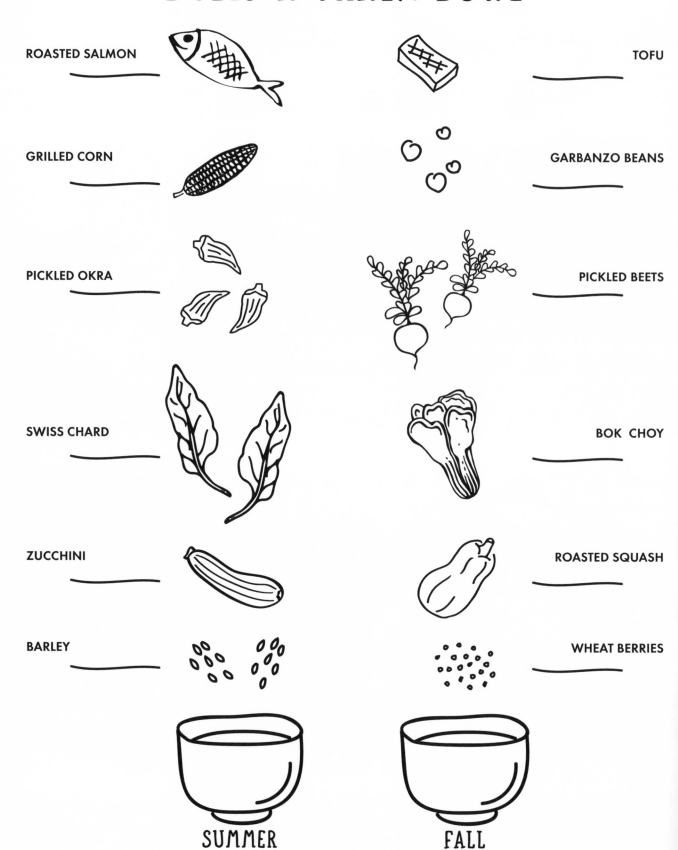

ROASTED SALMON

TOFU

GRILLED CORN

GARBANZO BEANS

PICKLED OKRA

PICKLED BEETS

SWISS CHARD

BOK CHOY

ZUCCHINI

ROASTED SQUASH

BARLEY

WHEAT BERRIES

SUMMER

FALL

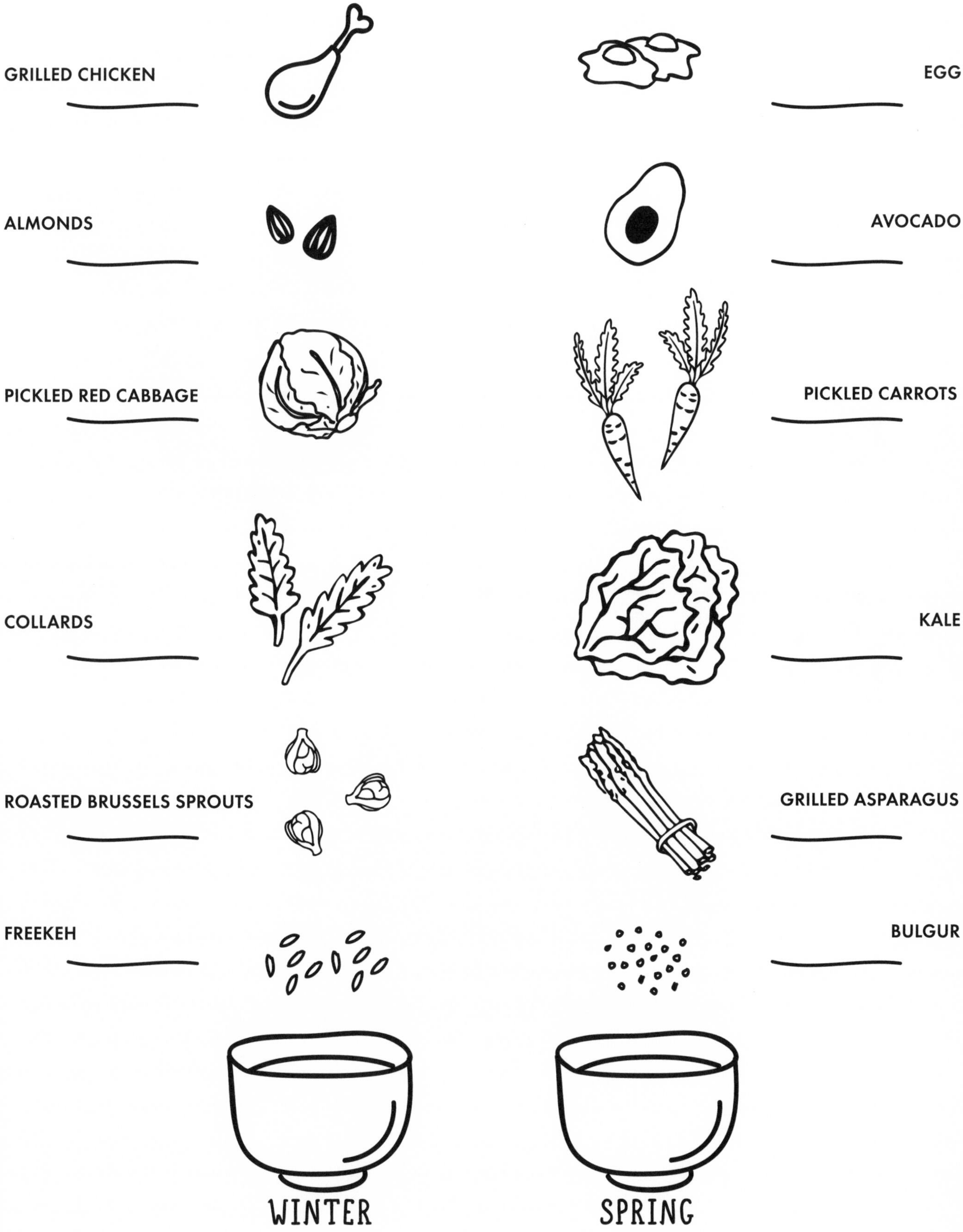

GRILLED CHICKEN
_____

EGG
_____

ALMONDS
_____

AVOCADO
_____

PICKLED RED CABBAGE
_____

PICKLED CARROTS
_____

COLLARDS
_____

KALE
_____

ROASTED BRUSSELS SPROUTS
_____

GRILLED ASPARAGUS
_____

FREEKEH
_____

BULGUR
_____

WINTER

SPRING

MUSTARD SEED-CRUSTED TOFU

Yields 4 servings

This is an excellent recipe for vegetarians and carnivores alike. The mustard seed crust provides a crunchy texture to the outside of the soft tofu and the spaghetti squash offers a starchy base to this dish. Feel free to add a scoop of red quinoa from our Maya's Grain Bowl (page 117) for extra protein.

1 (14-ounce) package extra firm tofu

½ cup soy sauce

1 tablespoon sriracha chili sauce

1 tablespoon sesame oil

1 spaghetti squash

3 to 4 tablespoons olive oil

Kosher salt

¼ cup ground mustard seeds

3 garlic cloves

¼ cup fresh parsley leaves

Preheat the oven to 350°F. Drain the tofu and cut across into 4 equal pieces. In a medium bowl, mix the soy sauce, sriracha chili sauce, and sesame oil. Submerge the tofu and marinate for 1 hour, turning once or twice.

Cut the squash in half lengthwise, and scoop and discard all the seeds from the center. Arrange the squash in a baking dish, cut sides facing up. Drizzle with olive oil and sprinkle a little salt into the cavities. Fill the bottom of the dish with ½ inch of water and cover with aluminum foil. Bake for 35 to 45 minutes, or until the flesh is soft and easily pierced with a knife. Allow the squash to cool. Once cooled, use a fork to comb the flesh of the squash, which should resemble spaghetti. Set aside.

Spread the ground mustard seeds onto a plate. Remove the tofu from the marinade and press the top and bottom sides into the ground mustard seeds until coated. Set aside.

Finely mince the garlic cloves. Coarsely chop the parsley leaves. In a large sauté pan over medium heat, heat 2 tablespoons of the olive oil. Add the garlic to the pan and toast to a light golden color. Add the squash and cook for 2 to 3 minutes, stirring often. Finish by adding the parsley and season with salt. Divide the squash among 4 plates.

In a nonstick pan, add enough olive oil to coat the bottom and heat over medium-high heat. Carefully place 1 or 2 pieces of tofu in the pan at a time, being careful not to overcrowd the pan. Toast both sides of the tofu until the tofu has a golden color. If they are taking on too much color, turn the heat down. A fish spatula works best to turn the tofu. Place each piece of tofu on top of the spaghetti squash for serving.

BLOODY MARY MUSSELS

Yields 2 servings

This is a bold and spicy preparation for mussels, borrowing from the favorite brunch classic. Fresh horseradish gives it a nasal-clearing kick, while the celery lends a bit of freshness.

1 lemon

1 (28-ounce) can whole peeled tomatoes

1 tablespoon Worcestershire sauce

½ teaspoon black pepper

½ teaspoon celery salt

1 tablespoon Hot Sauce (page 18), optional

1 piece fresh horseradish, roughly 4 inches long

2 pounds mussels

3 garlic cloves

2 celery stalks

1 tablespoon olive oil

Kosher salt

¼ cup white wine

Toasted baguette, for serving

Cut the lemon into quarters, removing the seeds. In a blender, combine the tomatoes, Worcestershire sauce, black pepper, celery salt, juice from 2 lemon wedges, and hot sauce (if using); blend until smooth.

Peel the horseradish and grate using a Microplane, add to the blender, and blend again until just combined.

Clean the mussels by rinsing them under cold water and pulling off any beards. If you spot any open mussels, discard them.

Mince the garlic and slice the celery across into ¼-inch half-moons. In a large pot over high heat, add the olive oil, garlic, and celery, stirring until the garlic begins to toast. Add the mussels, stirring to combine with the garlic and celery. Season with salt, add the white wine, and cover to allow the mussels to open, 3 to 5 minutes. Once opened, add the sauce to the pot of mussels and stir to combine. Cook for 1 to 2 minutes to allow sauce to heat up, and give one last stir to incorporate all the sauce from the bottom of the pan.

Serve with a toasted baguette and the remaining 2 lemon wedges.

PERI PERI CHICKEN WINGS

Yields 4 to 6 servings

During the first months of their relationship, Dean and Maya shared a plate of poussin rotisserie after work one night, laughing as they tore into it with their hands. Whenever there's the simple, joyful opportunity to eat messy chicken wings, to this day they'll dig in hands first with nostalgia. These chicken wings are baked first and then fried to ensure tender and moist meat. If you do not care to fry them, they can be served roasted with the Peri Peri Sauce.

2 tablespoons olive oil, plus more, for frying

6 tablespoons Peri Peri Spice (page 19)

2 garlic cloves, minced

1 teaspoon kosher salt, plus more as needed

2 pounds chicken wings

2 cups buttermilk

2 cups flour

2 tablespoons red wine vinegar

Peri Peri Sauce (recipe follows)

In a large bowl, combine the olive oil, 2 tablespoons of the peri peri spice, the garlic, and the salt. Add the wings and toss to coat. Let the wings marinate in the refrigerator for at least 1 hour—but 1 day is best.

Preheat the oven to 350°F. Roast the wings in a baking dish for 45 minutes, turning once while cooking. Let cool. Once the wings are cooled, pour the buttermilk over, tossing the wings so they are completely coated. Store in the refrigerator.

In a cast-iron pan, heat 2 inches of olive oil over medium-low heat to 325 to 350°F. Combine the flour and remaining 4 tablespoons peri peri spice in a bowl. Take one chicken wing at a time out of the buttermilk, allowing the excess buttermilk to drip off. Dredge each wing in the flour mixture and set aside on a plate until each wing is well coated in flour. Carefully place the wings into the hot oil, being careful not to overcrowd the pan. Once golden brown, turn each wing to cook the other side. Drain the wings on a plate lined with a paper towel and salt lightly.

To serve, whisk red wine vinegar with Peri Peri Sauce. Cover the wings with the sauce and toss lightly, or serve the sauce on the side for dipping.

PERI PERI SAUCE

Yields 2 cups

1 small yellow onion

3 garlic cloves

1 tablespoon olive oil

1 (14.5-ounce) can chopped tomatoes

2 tablespoons plus 1 teaspoon Peri Peri Spice (page 19)

1 teaspoon kosher salt, plus more if needed

1 tablespoon butter

1 tablespoon flour

¼ cup chicken stock

Finely mince half the yellow onion and the garlic cloves. In a medium sauté pan over low heat, heat the olive oil, onion, and garlic. Sweat for 5 to 8 minutes, until the onion and garlic are very soft and translucent.

While the vegetables are cooking, puree the tomatoes in a blender. Once the onion and garlic have softened, add the Peri Peri Spice and mix to combine. Add the pureed tomatoes and salt to the onion mix, mixing well to combine. If you would like a spicier sauce, add an extra teaspoon or two of peri peri spice to the sauce at this time. Simmer for 10 minutes so the flavors meld.

In a separate small sauté pan or saucepan, heat the butter over low heat until melted, add the flour, and stir to combine. Turn up the heat to medium and add the chicken stock. Stir continuously until the mixture has thickened and comes to a boil. Add the thickened stock to the peri peri mixture, stir well, and turn off the heat. If any lumps remain, cool slightly and return it to the blender and puree. Taste the sauce and season with salt if needed.

DRINKS AT JACK'S WIFE FREDA

For the longest time, the sleepy stretch of Lafayette Street between Spring and Broome in SoHo bordered a charming, small park planted in the middle of the busy intersection, but offered no real reprieve from how polarizing and lonely the city can feel. Sure, if you were hungry you'd grab a sandwich or a really solid plate of pasta, and in that way, you were satisfied. But there you were standing on a busy block of downtown New York and not an ally in sight.

Where was the community? The friendship! So much of what defines a good meal is who you get to share it with and where you eat it. At Jack's Wife Freda, you've got the best friendship baked into the managers and waiters, and Dean and Maya have an almost parent-like affection for their customers.

I know this to be true because when Jack's Wife opened in 2012, it almost immediately became my extended living room. The food was great—that's a given—but it had nothing to do with why I spent so much time there. I'd arrive at 6 P.M. to meet my girlfriends. 6 P.M. would become 9 P.M. would become closing at 11, and they'd never ask us to leave. On the contrary—just whether we needed more wine. Sometimes a manager or owner would sit down and join us and with the liquid confidence and stimulus imparted by a few glasses of wine, we'd talk about life and how to believe in ourselves, what dream-chasing means—perfect at-home dinner-party chatter, re-created in someone else's kitchen.

On some nights, I didn't even make plans. I'd just show up, ask for a cappuccino or a glass of the house chenin blanc and watch people come in, walk by, step out. Or so I thought. The thing about Jack's Wife is that almost immediately it became a new community. Lafayette Street strangers became friends, siblings, partners, and mentors. The restaurant experience, especially in New York, can often feel transactional—there is always someone waiting outside for your table—yet somehow Jack's Wife, even with its infamous long wait lines, has retained the spirit of not just a neighborhood joint that welcomes with a smile anyone who's willing to stop in, but has gone so far as to make you feel like family.

—Leandra Medine

BOOTSY COLLINS

Yields 1 cocktail

Our bartender, Jose, concocted this refreshing drink in namesake (and magenta) tribute to the bass-playing legend of funk. This is a take on a Tom Collins—replacing the traditional gin with vodka and using the French spirit Lillet to add an electric pink hue and slightly sweeten.

2 ounces good-quality vodka

1 ounce simple syrup

1 ounce fresh lemon juice

½ ounce Lillet Rouge

Ice

Club soda

Fresh mint, for garnish

In a cocktail shaker, combine the vodka, simple syrup, lemon juice, and Lillet Rouge.

Add a scoop of ice and vigorously shake.

Strain the vodka mixture into a tall glass filled with ice; the vodka mixture should only fill about one-half to three-quarters of the glass.

Finish by topping off the drink with club soda.

Fresh mint makes a great garnish to this refreshing drink.

JACK'S WIFE FREDA PIMM'S CUP

Yields 1 cocktail

This quintessential British cocktail is updated at the restaurant with fresh ginger for added zing—the perfect antidote to a humid summer night. Whether enjoying it from the stands at Wimbledon, at a sidewalk table at Jack's Wife Freda, or at home when you just need a reminder of what summer tastes like, this drink will not disappoint!

Ingredients	Instructions
1 (1-inch) piece fresh ginger	Cut the ginger into 2 thin slices and add to a cocktail shaker with the cucumber.
2 thin slices seedless cucumber	
½ ounce Mint Syrup (page 79)	Lightly muddle the ginger and cucumber with the Mint Syrup and lemon juice.
½ ounce fresh lemon juice	
3 ounces Pimm's No. 1	Add the Pimm's along with ice cubes to fill halfway, and shake vigorously.
Ice	Pour the contents of the shaker into a tall glass filled with ice, making sure not to strain out the cucumber or ginger.
Club soda	Top with club soda and stir gently.
Fresh mint, lemon wheel, and cucumber slice, for garnish	Garnish with a sprig of mint, a lemon wheel, and a cucumber slice.

THE PINK GUZZLER

Yields 1 cocktail

A pretty-in-pink summer refresher, this cocktail uses sweet watermelon juice. You can easily make your own by cutting a ripe watermelon into small cubes, making sure to discard all the seeds. Place in a blender and puree until completely smooth, then pour the juice through a fine-mesh strainer. The cayenne balances this sweet drink with a pinch of earthiness.

2 tablespoons kosher salt

2 tablespoons sugar

1 lime wedge

2 ounces good-quality tequila

1½ ounces fresh watermelon juice

½ ounce fresh lime juice

½ ounce simple syrup

Dash cayenne pepper

1 small wedge watermelon or lime, for garnish

In a small bowl, combine the salt and sugar.

Cut into the flesh of the wedge of lime and place it on the rim of a large rocks glass or margarita glass. Run the lime around the rim of the glass until it is completely dampened with the juice from the lime. Turn the glass upside down and dip it into the sugar mixture so that it adheres to the rim.

In a cocktail shaker, combine the tequila, watermelon juice, lime juice, simple syrup, and a dash of cayenne pepper. Fill with ice and shake vigorously. Pour the contents of the shaker into the glass and garnish with a small wedge of watermelon or lime.

MELON MIMOSA

Yields 4 portions

This take on the classic brunch cocktail uses our homemade cantaloupe juice.

4 ounces Lillet Blanc

4 ounces Cantaloupe Juice (page 78)

Champagne or other sparkling wine

Combine the Lillet Blanc and Cantaloupe Juice.

Measure 2 ounces of the cantaloupe mixture into each of four champagne flutes.

Top each flute with champagne.

JOSE'S HOT TODDY

Yields 1 drink

A balm for those snowy, windy, cold New York nights. Jose lovingly prepares a version of this toddy for sniffling friends, so if you're feeling under the weather, replace the bourbon with a dash of cayenne pepper, one whole unpeeled clove of garlic, and a touch of extra honey for his secret cure for the common cold.

1 navel orange

2 ounces good-quality bourbon

1 tablespoon honey

½ ounce fresh lemon juice

2 whole star anise

1 (2-inch) piece fresh ginger

Hold the navel orange firmly and use a vegetable peeler to peel off a large strip of zest.

Place the bourbon, honey, lemon juice, star anise, ginger, and orange peel in a heatproof glass.

Fill with boiling water and stir well to combine.

BLOODY MARY

Yields approximately 6 cups of mixer or 8 to 10 cocktails

This staple often takes a back seat during the brunch hours to some of our more brightly colored beverages, but it's a drink that carries many a vistor from breakfast into lunch and every once in a while straight into dinner. Jose's recipe makes a pitcher of Bloody Mary mix, so invite a crowd!

1 (46-ounce) can tomato juice

¾ cup freshly squeezed lemon juice

¼ cup freshly ground horseradish

2 tablespoons Worcestershire sauce

1 teaspoon Dijon mustard

1 teaspoon cayenne pepper

2 teaspoons black pepper

2 teaspoons kosher salt

2 teaspoons celery salt

2 tablespoons white wine vinegar

High-quality vodka, for serving

Olives, and lemon or lime wedges or slices, for garnish

Combine all ingredients and mix well. Check for seasoning and add more kosher salt if needed.

In a tumbler or highball glass, pour 2 ounces of your preferred vodka over ice, and add ¼ to ½ cup of the tomato mixer until it's balanced to your taste. Garnish with olives and a lemon or lime wedge or slice.

NEW YORK SOUR

Yields 1 cocktail

Legend has it that this handsome whiskey sour cocktail became New York–specific when its popularity soared during Prohibition—as the traditional speakeasy recipe called for lots of sugar, lemon, and wine to mask the terrible quality of the bootlegged whiskey. We borrow the Honey Syrup from our pancake recipe in lieu of sugar, and use a nice port for the depth it adds when swirled with the whiskey. Such a beautiful cocktail to sip in the autumn as the leaves start to change to the same color as the ruby red float.

2 ounces good-quality rye whiskey

½ ounce Honey Syrup (page 53)

1 ounce fresh lemon juice

Ice

1 to 2 tablespoons ruby port

Half slice of navel orange, for garnish

In a cocktail shaker, combine the rye, Honey Syrup, and lemon juice with a scoop of ice and shake vigorously.

Strain the drink into a rocks glass filled with ice.

Gently add the ruby port to the top of the cocktail, trying to keep the port floating on top of the drink.

Garnish with the half slice of navel orange.

HOME AWAY FROM HOME

New York is a city of small apartments, and smaller kitchens, so at the end of the day in the skyscrapers, I head to 50 Carmine Street. My family and I have been eating at Jack's Wife Freda since the day it opened. I love every meal, from the cantaloupe juice first thing in the morning to the malva pudding at the end of a birthday dinner.

When Jack's Wife Freda opened, my grandma Charlotte was 101 years old. She lived in Florida and couldn't travel far. But she had serious FOMO about not going to the opening-night party. On my way to visit her soon after, I stopped at Jack's and asked Dean for one of everything on the menu to go, so I could take it to Grandma. All of it: Freda's Liver and Onions, Peri Peri Chicken Wings, containers of Greek salad, Prego Rolls, mussels, matzo ball soup in a container I could put in my checked bag (no liquids through security!). We packed everything in the suitcase, stuffing sweatshirts around the containers and crossing our fingers. Spiced beet dip is not something you want to come flying out of the baggage carousel. That evening, at her own kitchen table with family around her, Grandma tasted the grilled haloumi and grapes first. She smiled, then picked up the menu I'd brought and said with a twinkle, "Let's see . . . what'll I have next?" It was the best restaurant dinner my family has ever eaten together.

But my favorite meal at Jack's is a late-night snack. When I'm acting in a play, I sneak out the stage door when the curtain falls and go downtown. Maya, Dean, or Oliver will be choreographing the swirl of conversation and late suppers in the golden-lit dining room and bar full of flowers. The Freda's Negroni and Zucchini Chips are a must. Get two orders of Zucchini Chips, 'cause they disappear fast, and New Yorkers like to eat while they talk.

One night, after being away for several months, I landed in New York and said to the cab driver at the airport, "Lafayette and Spring Street, please." Jack's windows were twinkling, Dean rolled my suitcase into the kitchen (and it's a pretty small kitchen), and I plunked myself down in a corner booth. As soon as the Zucchini Chips and a Negroni hit the table, I was home.

—Piper Perabo

SPICED BEET DIP

Yields 2 to 3 cups

This is a great recipe for entertaining as it can be made ahead of time and can sit out for quite a while. Plus, its beautiful rich magenta color is a showstopper. The natural sweetness of the beets is balanced by the nuttiness of the tahini in this unexpected alternative to standard hummus. It's best served with toasted pita triangles or chips.

1½ pounds beets (roughly 3 medium beets)

8 garlic cloves

¼ cup plus 2 tablespoons extra-virgin olive oil

¼ cup tahini

Juice of ½ lemon

½ teaspoon kosher salt

1 tablespoon za'atar

2 tablespoons crumbled feta

Pita, for serving

Preheat the oven to 350°F. Peel the beets and cut into quarters. In a small bowl, toss with the garlic and 2 tablespoons olive oil and place in a baking dish. Cover with aluminum foil and roast for 30 minutes. The beets will be very tender when a small knife is inserted in the middle (be sure to test out a few larger pieces); if the beets are not easily pierced, roast for an additional 10 to 15 minutes and test again.

Once the beets and garlic cool slightly, place them in a food processor and process until combined. Add the tahini, lemon juice, and salt and blend again, scraping any bits off the sides. Process again, pouring the remaining ¼ cup olive oil in a slow stream into the food processor while the mixture is blending. Once all the ingredients are added, process for 3 minutes or until the mixture is very smooth. Transfer to a plate for serving or into a container and refrigerate.

To serve, sprinkle za'atar over the dip, add the crumbled feta cheese on top, and finish with a hefty splash of extra-virgin olive oil. Serve with pita for dipping.

HALOUMI WITH GRAPES

Yields 2 to 4 servings

The Greeks claim it on their mezze menus, the Cypriotes make it, and it's a favorite snack throughout the Mediterranean. Haloumi's very high melting point makes it the perfect grilling cheese. We especially love its saltiness paired with the sweet-and-sour tartness of grapes. Drizzle with a high-quality extra-virgin olive oil to finish.

½ cup green grapes, cut in half lengthwise

½ cup red or black grapes, cut in half lengthwise

1 garlic clove, minced

2 tablespoons olive oil

Kosher salt

1 package haloumi (8 to 9 ounces)

1 tablespoon packed chopped fresh mint leaves

1 to 2 tablespoons extra-virgin olive oil

Place the grapes in a small bowl with the garlic, 1 tablespoon of the olive oil, and a pinch of salt.

Cut the haloumi crosswise into ½-inch-thick slices. Heat a cast-iron or nonstick pan over high heat. Once hot, add the remaining 1 tablespoon olive oil and sear each piece of haloumi on each side until golden brown (20 to 30 seconds per side). Arrange in a line on a platter, overlapping slightly.

Once the haloumi is cooked, keep the sauté pan on high heat and cook the grapes and garlic for 2 minutes, or just until the color of the grapes begins to fade. Spoon the grapes on top of the haloumi. Finish with chopped mint and extra-virgin olive oil.

ZUCCHINI CHIPS

Yields 4 to 6 servings

Our staff generally agrees that the Zucchini Chips are one of the most addictive dishes on the menu—consider yourself warned. These chips are delicious as an appetizer or side dish for dinner. We serve them with our Smoked Paprika Aioli, although if you're looking for something lighter and zestier, our Hot Sauce (page 18)—as usual—does the trick.

3 medium green zucchini

1 cup flour

1 tablespoon cornstarch

1 teaspoon kosher salt, plus more as needed

1¼ cups seltzer water

2 cups panko bread crumbs

2 cups vegetable oil

Smoked Paprika Aioli (page 20)

Rinse the zucchini and cut across on a slight angle into ¼-inch-thick slices.

In a large bowl, combine the flour, cornstarch, and salt. Slowly whisk in the seltzer water.

Place the panko bread crumbs in a separate large bowl. Using one hand for the wet mixture and one hand for the dry, dip the zucchini into the wet batter, using the side of the bowl to wipe off any excess, and place in the panko. Coat all sides of the zucchini thoroughly with the panko. Place on a baking sheet and continue with the rest of the zucchini.

In a deep saucepan, heat the vegetable oil over medium heat to roughly 350°F. Fry the zucchini on each side until golden in color, transfer to a plate lined with paper towels, and salt lightly.

Place the Smoked Paprika Aioli in a small bowl, whisking in 1 or 2 tablespoons cold water if needed to thin the aioli slightly. Serve the zucchini chips with Smoked Paprika Aoili for dipping.

Flourless Chipotle Chocolat
asonal Bake

LAMB TARTARE

Yields 2 to 4 servings

This spiced tartare does not use an egg yolk like most, instead adding a hefty dose of olive oil. Since this dish is served raw, seek out very high-quality lamb. It is best to put the loin into the freezer for 10 or 15 minutes to allow for easier handling.

6 ounces lamb loin

1 tablespoon capers

1 teaspoon ground cumin

1 teaspoon ground coriander

1 tablespoon packed fresh mint leaves

½ lemon

1 teaspoon Dijon mustard

1 teaspoon sriracha chili sauce

½ teaspoon kosher salt, plus more if needed

1 tablespoon olive oil, plus more for serving

Microgreens, for garnish

Toasted pita, for serving

If your lamb loin happens to be on the bone, cut the meat from the bone. Trim any silver skin that may be on the meat. Cut the loin into ¼-inch strips. Taking one strip at a time, cut lengthwise once again into ¼-inch strips. Gather all the strips and cut across into very small cubes. Gather all the meat and run your knife over it multiple times until the meat is finely chopped. Place in a bowl and refrigerate.

Meanwhile, rinse the capers under cold water, dry slightly, and chop well. Mix the cumin and coriander together. Finely mince the mint leaves. Cut the lemon into quarters and remove any seeds. Once the meat has chilled, squeeze the lemon directly onto the meat. Follow by adding the spices, capers, mint, Dijon mustard, sriracha, salt, and olive oil. Stir the tartare very well until all the ingredients are incorporated. Taste for salt, adding more if needed.

Plate the tartare and drizzle with additional olive oil. Garnish with microgreens and serve with toasted pita.

ROASTED CAULIFLOWER

Yields 2 to 4 servings

Cauliflower is truly the star in this recipe that highlights both the cooked and raw preparations of a hearty cold weather vegetable. Choose heads that are firm and tightly closed with a pale white color. The lemon-garlic dressing and fried capers give this a burst of flavor. Feel free to try the dressing, which will keep in the refrigerator for up to a week, on other vegetables, served with crudités, or tossed with a salad as well.

1 head cauliflower

1¼ cups plus 2 tablespoons olive oil

Kosher salt

¼ cup capers

¼ cup packed fresh parsley leaves

¼ cup fresh lemon juice

3 garlic cloves

1 egg yolk

1 tablespoon Dijon mustard

1 tablespoon Worcestershire sauce

¼ cup grated Parmesan cheese

Cracked black pepper

Preheat the oven to 425°F. Quarter the cauliflower and cut out the ribs. Set one quarter of the cauliflower aside. Break the rest of the cauliflower into large florets roughly the same size. If any florets are too large, cut in half with a knife. Toss the florets in a large bowl with 2 tablespoons of the olive oil and a few pinches of salt. Spread the cauliflower on a baking sheet and bake for 20 to 25 minutes, turning the cauliflower halfway through the cooking process, until browned and cooked to your liking.

In a sauté pan over medium heat, heat ¼ cup of the olive oil, and fry the capers, shaking the pan often to cook evenly. Do take care since capers may burst and sometimes jump out of the pan. You may want to cover the pan with a lid. Once the capers are light brown and toasted, strain and allow them to drain on a few pieces of paper towel.

Cut the remaining quarter of cauliflower across into very thin slices, using only the florets and not the stem. Coarsely chop the parsley leaves. Combine the raw cauliflower, parsley, and fried capers in a small bowl.

In a blender or food processor, blend the lemon juice, garlic, egg yolk, Worcestershire sauce, and mustard until combined. While the blender is running, slowly add the remaining 1 cup olive oil in a slow, steady stream. If the consistency is too thick, add 1 tablespoon water. Add the Parmesan and blend until combined. Transfer the dressing to a small bowl and season with pepper.

To assemble the dish, spoon ¼ cup of the dressing into a thin layer covering the bottom of your serving dish. Place the cooked cauliflower on top of the dressing in an even layer. Dress the raw cauliflower salad with 3 to 4 tablespoons of the dressing or until well coated. Salt to taste. Spread the raw cauliflower salad on top of the cooked cauliflower. Feel free to garnish with additional parsley and cracked pepper.

LAMB KEFTA

Yields 14 to 16 keftas

These lamb "meatballs" have a wonderfully aromatic smell and taste. They are served with a nutty tahini sauce and topped with sweet currants and pine nuts. Since they are made of lamb, it is only necessary to sear the outside of the kefta, leaving the middle slightly pink and moist. They can be made ahead of time and kept in the refrigerator overnight before cooking.

½ yellow onion

2 garlic cloves

1 pound ground lamb

2 teaspoons ground cumin

½ teaspoon ground cinnamon

½ teaspoon ground allspice

¼ teaspoon ground cloves

Kosher salt

½ cup chopped fresh parsley

¼ cup chicken stock or water

¼ cup bread crumbs

¼ cup pine nuts

2 tablespoons currants or raisins

½ cup tahini

¼ cup plus 1 tablespoon olive oil

3 tablespoons fresh lemon juice

Pinch of cayenne

Grate the onion on the largest holes of a box grater, then place in a large bowl. Mince the garlic and add to the bowl with the onion. Add the ground lamb, cumin, cinnamon, allspice, cloves, 1 teaspoon salt, and ¼ cup of the parsley and mix with clean hands until thoroughly combined.

Heat the chicken stock or water and add to the bread crumbs, stirring to combine. Add the bread crumb mixture to the lamb and once again mix with your hands until everything is well combined.

Spoon out a heaping tablespoon (roughly 1½ ounces) of the lamb mixture and roll it into a ball, then roll it back and forth between your hands to create an oval, egglike shape. Repeat with the remaining lamb mixture. You should end up with 14 to 16 kefta. Refrigerate for at least 15 minutes or up to 1 day, so that the lamb firms up.

While the meat is resting, toast the pine nuts in a small sauté pan over low heat. Swirl them in the pan constantly until they begin to take on a golden color, then transfer to a plate to cool.

Put the remaining ¼ cup parsley in a small bowl. Coarsely chop the currants and add to the bowl with the parsley. Once the pine nuts have cooled slightly, coarsely chop them and add to the bowl with the currants and parsley, mixing all to combine; set aside.

In a blender, blend the tahini, ½ cup water, ¼ cup of the olive oil, the lemon juice, and the cayenne. Season with salt and add additional water if the mixture is too thick.

In a cast-iron pan or large skillet over medium heat, heat the remaining 1 tablespoon olive oil. Add the keftas side by side, not overcrowding the pan. You may have to sear them in two batches. Cook the keftas on all sides for 4 to 6 minutes, until they are nicely browned and the meat is slightly underdone in the center. Transfer to a plate and allow to cool slightly.

Liberally coat the bottom of your serving platter or plate with the tahini sauce. Place the keftas on top of the tahini, and finish by garnishing with a few handfuls of pine nuts and currants.

DURBAN MUSSELS

Yields 2 to 4 servings

"We need a dish that smells like Durban!" said Dean one day.

The Jankelowitz family used to vacation in the coastal South African city during the summertime, and Dean remembers it dreamily for the elegant beachfront hotels and the best Indian food outside of India. After some research, Chef Julia began to conjure the smell of fennel, curry, and salt water in the air. She got to work tinkering with various ingredients and flavors, and finally served this very same bowl of mussels to Dean, who smiled and said, "Smells just like home." This recipe makes enough for four as an appetizer or dinner for two. We serve it with crusty toasted bread made with a little of our garlic butter for a more substantial meal.

1 head fennel

1 small yellow onion

5 garlic cloves

2 tablespoons olive oil

2 tablespoons curry powder

1 teaspoon ground coriander

1 teaspoon ground turmeric

1 teaspoon paprika

½ teaspoon ground fennel seed

½ teaspoon kosher salt, plus more as needed

2 tablespoons butter

2 pounds mussels

½ cup white wine

Cut any green stalks off the fennel and discard any outer discolored layers if present. Coarsely chop into large pieces. Peel the onion and also coarsely chop into large pieces. Coarsely chop 2 garlic cloves, being careful not to mince them too finely.

In a medium saucepan, combine 1 tablespoon of the olive oil, the fennel bulb, onion, and chopped garlic. Sauté over medium-low heat until the vegetables begin to soften, roughly 10 minutes. Once soft, add the curry, coriander, turmeric, paprika, ground fennel, and ¼ teaspoon of the salt. Stir to coat all the vegetables with the spices. Add 2 cups water, turn the heat down to low, and simmer for 5 minutes.

Transfer everything to a blender and blend on high speed for 1 to 2 minutes, adding an additional 1/4 cup water and 1 tablespoon of the butter. Pour the mixture through a fine-mesh strainer. The mixture should be very smooth, similar to a soup. Season with salt and set aside while preparing the mussels.

Wash the mussels with very cold water and pull off any beards. If you spot any open mussels, discard them. Mince the remaining 3 garlic cloves. In a very large pot over medium heat, heat the remaining 1 tablespoon olive oil and the garlic. Immediately add the mussels with the remaining ½ teaspoon salt, stirring to combine with the garlic. Add the white wine and cover the mussels for 2 to 3 minutes. Lift the lid and stir; the mussels should be starting to open. Add 1 cup of the fennel sauce and the remaining 1 tablespoon butter and cover.

After 2 minutes stir again; almost all the mussels should be open. If they are not, return the lid and cook for an additional 2 to 3 minutes. Once most of the shells are open, transfer the mussels to a large bowl, pouring all the liquid on top of the mussels. If you prefer additional sauce, reheat and pour over the mussels.

CHICKEN LIVERS ON TOAST

Yields 2 servings

Though it may sound unusual, chicken livers are Maya's childhood comfort food. At eight years old, Maya had just moved to Israel with her family and she hardly spoke the language, but she managed to make her first childhood friend—a girl who always invited her over for playdates after school. The girl's mother would prepare chicken livers weekly, and the two new friends would sit around the table snacking and giggling—a tradition that has lasted to this day. Chicken livers are an old-world delicacy being brought back today mostly in the form of pâté. This recipe, however, uses the whole liver, adding port wine and caramelized onions to give a slightly sweet, rich sauce. If you prefer a stronger liver flavor, omit the buttermilk step and bread the livers directly with the flour after rinsing with cold water.

1 small yellow onion

4 tablespoons olive oil

1 teaspoon kosher salt, plus more as needed

4 ounces chicken livers

1 cup buttermilk

½ cup flour

1 tablespoon Peri Peri Spice (page 19)

½ cup port wine

¼ to ½ cup chicken stock

1 tablespoon butter

2 thick slices sourdough bread

Peel the onion, cut in half, and then cut across into thin slices. In a sauté pan over medium-high heat, heat 1 tablespoon of the olive oil and the sliced onion. Stir the onion continuously until it has a golden color, turn the heat down to low, and cook for an additional 20 to 25 minutes, stirring often. The onion should have a deep brown, caramelized color. Season with salt.

Clean the livers by cutting off any connective veins, rinse under cold water, dry on a piece of paper towel, and transfer to a small bowl. Add the buttermilk to the livers and let soak for at least 15 minutes.

In a mixing bowl, add flour, Peri Peri Spice, and 1 teaspoon salt, stirring to combine. Heat the remaining 3 tablespoons olive oil in a sauté pan over medium-high heat. Coat each piece of liver in the seasoned flour and sauté on each side until golden brown in color.

Once the livers are cooked, transfer to a plate. Discard any extra olive oil in the pan and turn the heat up to high. Working quickly, add the port and allow to reduce by a third. Add the chicken stock and butter and reduce by half, adding the onion halfway through the cooking process. Once the liquid has reduced, taste and add additional salt if needed.

Toast the sourdough bread and place in the middle of a serving plate. Divide the livers in half and place on the toast in a row. Spoon the onion and sauce over all before serving.

JALAPEÑO AND GRUYÈRE PASTA

Yields 4 to 6 portions

This pasta is our version of a spicy, grown-up mac and cheese! Jalapeños can have different levels of heat but cooking them will mellow the flavor a bit. If you prefer more spice, add additional raw sliced jalapeños to garnish before eating.

3 jalapeño chilies

8 garlic cloves

1 (16-ounce) box orecchiete

2 tablespoons olive oil

½ cup white wine

4 tablespoons (½ stick) butter

2 cups shredded Gruyère cheese

¼ cup kosher salt

Slice the jalapeños across into thin rounds and finely mince the garlic. Set aside the garlic and jalapeños. Bring 5 quarts water—salted to taste like the ocean!—to a boil. Add the pasta and cook for 9 minutes (the instructions on most packages say 13 minutes, although the pasta will absorb more liquid later, so stick to 9 minutes to avoid overcooking). Before straining the pasta, reserve ½ cup of the pasta water.

In the same pot used for cooking the pasta, combine the olive oil, garlic, and jalapeños. Cook over medium-low heat until the garlic begins to toast and the jalapeños soften. Add the white wine and butter. Once the butter has melted, return the pasta to the pot and stir. Add the shredded Gruyère cheese and reserved pasta water, a little at a time, until all the cheese has melted and the pasta appears creamy. Note: You may not use all of the reserved pasta water. Serve immediately with thinly sliced, fresh jalapeños on top if desired.

LAMB AND EGGPLANT LASAGNE

Yields 4 to 6 servings

This is a sumptuous and gluten-free recipe that uses slices of eggplant in lieu of pasta. Use a high-sided baking dish to keep in all the juices. It is a great make-ahead meal, as it can sit in the refrigerator for up to 3 days before baking. The pomodoro used here is a simple, versatile sauce that can be tossed with pasta as well for a quick dinner. It will keep for several days in the refrigerator.

1½ small yellow onions

6 garlic cloves

1 (28-ounce) can peeled tomatoes

½ cup plus 2 tablespoons extra-virgin olive oil

Pinch of chili flakes

Kosher salt

1 pound ground lamb

1 tablespoon Hungarian paprika

2 teaspoons ground cumin

2 teaspoons ground coriander

3 medium Italian eggplants

¼ cup balsamic vinegar

2 cups shredded mozzarella cheese

1 cup crumbled feta cheese

2 tablespoons chopped fresh parsley

To make the pomodoro sauce, finely mince or grate the small whole onion and 3 garlic cloves; reserve. Process the peeled tomatoes in a food processor until smooth and set aside. Heat ¼ cup of the olive oil in a saucepan over medium-low heat. Add the minced onion and cook, stirring often, until very soft, about 12 minutes. Add the garlic and cook, stirring often, for 2 to 4 minutes. Add the chili flakes; cook for 1 minute more. Add the pureed tomatoes and season lightly with salt; cook, stirring occasionally, until the sauce thickens slightly and the flavors meld, 15 to 20 minutes.

Mince the remaining 3 garlic cloves and yellow onion half. In a sauté pan over medium-high heat, sauté the onion in 2 tablespoons of the olive oil until it begins to soften, add the garlic and cook for another minute or two. Add the ground lamb and cook, breaking the meat up with a spatula. Once the meat is almost cooked through, add the spices and 2 teaspoons salt. Turn off the heat and stir in 1 cup pomodoro sauce. Season with salt.

Slice the eggplant across into circles roughly ½ inch thick. Salt both sides of the eggplant and drizzle with balsamic vinegar and the remaining olive oil, making sure each piece of eggplant is coated.

On a medium grill (or grill pan), cook the eggplant until both sides are nicely charred.

Once finished, place all the eggplant slices in a bowl and cover with plastic wrap.

Preheat the oven to 350°F. For best results use a deep 2½-quart casserole dish. Spread ½ cup of the pomodoro sauce on the bottom of the casserole dish. Line the bottom with half the eggplant in one even layer, trying to cover as much of the sauce as possible without overlapping the eggplant too much. Spread half the lamb mixture over the eggplant in an even layer. Cover the lamb with 1 cup of the mozzarella. Spread the remaining lamb on top of the cheese. Continue with another layer of eggplant. Cover the eggplant with the rest of the pomodoro sauce. Finish with the remaining 1 cup mozzarella. Cover with aluminum foil and bake for 30 minutes, or until the center is hot and the sauce is bubbling around the sides of the dish. Remove the foil and garnish with the feta and parsley.

DUCK TAGINE

Yields 4 portions

We use duck legs in our interpretation of this classic North African stew for added richness and depth to the spiced braising sauce. It's best to prep all the ingredients and have them ready to use while assembling this dish. You can simmer the tagine slowly on the stovetop or place it in a low-temperature oven to finish the braise. We serve this with couscous, which soaks up all the delicious flavors and adds a delicate, fluffy texture to the dish.

1 large yellow onion

5 garlic cloves

1 tablespoon chopped fresh ginger

½ cup prunes

½ cup dried apricots

¼ cup golden raisins

3 medium carrots

1 tablespoon ground coriander

2 teaspoons ground cumin

½ teaspoon ground cinnamon

¼ teaspoon cayenne

1 lemon

1 orange

4 duck legs

Kosher salt

1 tablespoon olive oil

5 cups chicken stock

1 tablespoon chopped fresh parsley

1 tablespoon chopped fresh mint

Couscous (page 105), for serving

Peel the onion and cut into medium dice. Mince the garlic and place the onion, garlic, and ginger in a small bowl. Cut the prunes in half, then across into ¼-inch pieces; follow with the apricots. Coarsely chop the raisins and combine all the dried fruit in a small bowl. Peel the carrots and cut in half lengthwise, then cut across into ½-inch half-moons.

Combine all the spices in a small bowl.

Zest the lemon and orange first, reserving the zest; follow by juicing each fruit. Combine the juice and zests in a small bowl.

Trim any fat from the sides of the duck legs and salt liberally on both sides. Heat a Dutch oven, large enough to hold all 4 legs comfortably, over high heat. Pour in the olive oil. Place all 4 legs in the pot, skin side down, and sear until dark golden brown. Turn down the heat and transfer the duck legs to a plate.

Discard all but 2 tablespoons of the fat in the pot, or enough to cover the bottom of the Dutch oven. Add the onion, garlic, and ginger, and sauté until the vegetables have softened, roughly 5 minutes. Add the spices and stir so the spices completely coat the vegetables.

Turn the heat to medium-high. Deglaze with the citrus juice-zest mixture and cook until all the liquid has evaporated. Add the dried fruits and chicken stock, and bring to a boil. Turn down to a simmer and gently place the duck legs, skin side up, back into the Dutch oven, making sure they are completely submerged in the liquid. Place the carrots on top and cover the Dutch oven. Either turn the stovetop to the lowest heat or place in a preheated 300°F oven for 2 hours. After 2 hours check to see if the duck legs are so tender that the meat easily begins to fall off the bone. If they are not yet tender, cook for an additional 20 to 30 minutes.

Carefully transfer the duck legs to a serving dish. Stir the cooking liquid, which should have thickened to a sauce. If it's not quite thick enough, return to medium heat and reduce for an additional 10 to 15 minutes. Pour the sauce over the meat and garnish with the chopped parsley and mint. Serve with couscous.

SWEETBREADS WITH PERI PERI SAUCE

Yields 4 servings

This recipe was inspired by Freda's famed chicken giblet recipe. At the restaurant, Julia suggested substituting the giblets with sweetbreads (the thymus gland of veal) for their burst of flavor and tender texture. The Peri Peri Sauce serves as a sort of gravy—the acidity and sweetness of the tomatoes highlight the richness of the meat.

1 pound sweetbreads

½ cup white wine vinegar

2 tablespoons kosher salt

1 cup buttermilk

1 cup vegetable oil

1 cup flour

1 tablespoon Peri Peri Spice (page 19)

1 cup Peri Peri Sauce (page 129)

Warm baguette, for serving

Rinse the sweetbreads under cold water. In a large stockpot, combine the sweetbreads, 2 quarts water, the vinegar, and the salt and bring to a boil; reduce to a simmer and cook for 10 minutes. Drain the sweetbreads and transfer to a bowl of ice water to cool. Once cooled, remove the membrane and any tubes you may see. Portion the sweetbreads into equal-size pieces and place in the buttermilk.

In a small saucepan, heat the Peri Peri Sauce and set aside. In a cast-iron pan, heat the oil over medium heat. In a medium bowl, mix the flour and Peri Peri Spice. Dredge each piece of sweetbread in the spiced flour. Fry the sweetbreads in the oil until golden in color on all sides. Transfer to a paper towel–lined plate.

To serve, divide the sweetbreads among four plates, spoon the desired amount of Peri Peri Sauce over the top, and serve with a warm baguette.

PERI PERI CHICKEN

Yields 2 to 4 servings

One of Dean's most formative food memories was the delight of devouring Peri Peri Chicken at Nando's first location in Johannesburg. When Jack's Wife Freda opened, it was imperative to Dean that the menu include a chicken dish just as memorable. Chef Julia's version is dry-rubbed in our Peri Peri Spice mix, pressed on the grill, and served in all its spicy, crispy, ultra-tender glory. Our Peri Peri Chicken just may be considered the "when in Rome" of Jack's Wife Freda! Serve with our refreshing Chopped Salad (page 193) and amp up the heat with our hot sauce alongside.

1 (3-pound) whole chicken

¼ cup olive oil

Kosher salt

¼ cup Peri Peri Spice (page 19)

Begin by halving the chicken. Starting at the breast, cut on the breastbone until you hit the plate, then slide your knife under the breast meat, cutting all the way to the wing. Cut under the wing so that it is attached to the breast. Continue cutting down the backbone until you reach the thigh bone. Once here, cut the point in between the thigh and the backbone to release the leg and continue cutting down toward the tail bone to release the chicken half. Once both the halves are separated you will be left with the carcass, which is excellent for making stock or our Matzo Ball Soup (page 87).

Rub the chicken halves with the olive oil and liberally salt each side. Thoroughly coat each side of the chicken with Peri Peri Spice. Let the seasoned chicken sit in the refrigerator for at least 1 hour, although overnight is best.

Preheat a grill. Grill on medium heat for 5 minutes over the hottest section of the grill to nicely brown each side. Move the chicken halves to the back or off to the side out of the direct heat to continue cooking for another 20 to 25 minutes, or until the juices run clear. You can also bake the chicken at 375°F for 30 to 40 minutes, depending on the size of the bird.

CHOPPED SALAD

Yields 4 servings/2 to 2½ cups

For young Maya in Israel, this salad was as ubiquitous at the table as salt and pepper. She calls it an Israeli Salad, and many call it an Arab Salad or Palestinian Salad—we simply call it a Chopped Salad. It is a versatile side that accompanies not only our Peri Peri Chicken (page 191) but also works during the morning hours with our Mediterranean breakfast of scrambled eggs with labneh and toasted pita. The crisp freshness of this salad is especially highlighted with luscious ripe tomatoes. It makes a great alternative to green salad or slaw with sandwiches, too.

1 English (hothouse) cucumber

3 plum tomatoes

1 small red onion

2 tablespoons packed fresh mint leaves

¼ cup packed fresh parsley leaves

Juice of ½ lemon

2 tablespoons extra-virgin olive oil

Kosher salt

Cut the cucumber in half, reserving one half for another use. Cut the cucumber half into a small dice, including the skin, and place in a medium bowl.

Cut the tomatoes in quarters, discarding the pulp and seeds in the middle, and cut the flesh and skin into a small dice.

Peel the red onion and cut in half, reserving half for another use. Cut the remaining half into a small dice.

Finely chop the mint and parsley and add to the vegetables. Add the lemon juice and olive oil and mix to combine. Season with salt.

SPICED RACK OF LAMB WITH ISRAELI COUSCOUS

Yields 2 servings

Few things gave Freda as much pride as going to the butcher and picking out the perfect rack of lamb. After seasoning it with her "magic spice" and serving it to the family, one thing became clear: there was no butcher in Johannesburg with a rack of lamb big enough to satisfy her family's appetite for her signature dish. At Jack's Wife Freda we pair our take on Freda's recipe with an Israeli couscous salad, brightened by fresh zesty lemon. When choosing from your butcher, we encourage you to look for locally raised lambs if possible. In the absence of a local option, we recommend substituting with lamb imported from Australia or New Zealand.

1 tablespoon ground coriander

1 tablespoon plus 1 teaspoon ground cumin

1 tablespoon za'atar

¼ teaspoon chili flakes

½ teaspoon smoked paprika

2 garlic cloves

2 tablespoons olive oil, plus more if needed

1 cup Israeli couscous

1¼ cups chicken stock

½ teaspoon kosher salt, plus more as needed

1 bay leaf

1 rack of lamb, trimmed

Black pepper

¼ cup finely chopped red onion

½ English (hothouse) cucumber

¼ cup packed fresh parsley leaves

¼ cup packed fresh mint leaves

¼ cup extra-virgin olive oil

Zest of ½ lemon

¼ cup fresh lemon juice

1 cup packed baby arugula

Mix the coriander, 1 tablespoon of the cumin, the za'atar, chili flakes, and smoked paprika in a small bowl and set aside. Mince the garlic and set aside.

In a large saucepan over medium heat, heat the olive oil and Israeli couscous. Stir continually to toast the couscous. Once the couscous starts toasting to a light golden brown, add the minced garlic and continue stirring for 1 minute. Add the chicken stock, salt, and bay leaf. Turn the heat down to low and cover. Cook until all the liquid has been absorbed by the couscous. Transfer the couscous to a bowl and allow to cool to room temperature.

While the couscous is cooling, prepare the lamb by cutting the rack in half between the fourth and fifth bone. Season the outside of the meat with salt and pepper. Place the spice mixture on a plate and press the lamb chops into it, rubbing the spice mix to completely coat each piece of lamb with the mixture.

Either on a very hot grill or in a cast-iron skillet coated with 2 tablespoons olive oil, cook all sides of the meat until it has reached the desired temperature. Lamb cooks quickly; for medium-rare, cook each side for 3 to 4 minutes. Once the meat is done, transfer to a plate and cover with aluminum foil.

Finely chop the red onion, and cut the cucumber, including the skin, in a medium slice, adding both to the couscous. Chop the parsley and mint finely and also add to the couscous with the remaining 1 teaspoon cumin, the extra-virgin olive oil, lemon zest, and juice. Stir well and check the couscous for seasoning, adding more salt if needed. Lastly add the baby arugula to the couscous and once again stir.

Serve the lamb chops on top of a bed of the couscous. We like a dollop of Tzatziki (page 20) on the side.

ENTREES

Durban Mussels
with fennel, coriander curry sauce and jus

Peri-Peri Chicken *with diced salad*

Fish a la Plancha *sesame soy glazed with kale and F*
fish head to tail

Maître D butter & F

10

FREDA'S FISHBALLS

Yields 15 to 18 pieces

Smoked whitefish and horseradish are used here in homage to Freda's and Maya's grandmothers' gefilte fish recipes. If you are having trouble finding smoked whitefish, smoked trout may be substituted. It's best to eat these after they are just cooked and piping-hot; once cooked, the fish will begin to firm up slightly.

1 small carrot

1 pound hake (cod can be substituted), cut into small cubes

6 ounces smoked whitefish

3 eggs

3 tablespoons heavy cream

1 small shallot, minced

3 garlic cloves, minced

¼ cup packed flat-leaf parsley leaves, chopped

Olive oil

1 to 2 cups sunflower seed oil or vegetable oil of choice

1 cup flour

2 cups panko bread crumbs

½ teaspoon kosher salt, plus more as needed

HORSERADISH MAYONAISE

1 (4-inch) piece fresh horseradish

1 recipe Homemade Mayonaise (page 18)

Cracked black pepper

Peel the carrot and cut in half. Working with one half at a time, cut the half into ¼-inch strips lengthwise. Take each strip and cut again lengthwise into ¼-inch strips. Gather all the ¼-inch strips and cut across into a very small dice, then repeat with the remaining half of the carrot.

Place the hake into a food processor. Add 1 egg, the heavy cream, and ½ teaspoon salt to the fish and process until smooth. Add the smoked whitefish and process again until combined.

Transfer the fish mixture to a large bowl, add the shallot, garlic, carrot, and parsley, and mix well.

Cover the fish mixture with plastic wrap and refrigerate for 30 minutes (the mixture will firm up and be easier to handle).

While fish chills, place the flour in a large bowl, the panko in a second large bowl, and the remaining 2 eggs in a third bowl. Whisk the eggs until well combined and the color is uniform.

Remove the fish mixture from the refrigerator. Roll 1 tablespoon of the chilled fish mixture into a ball. (If you find the fish is sticking to your hands, lightly grease your hands with olive oil.) Drop it into the flour and roll to coat completely. Roll each fishball in the egg until evenly coated, and then in the panko to coat.

In a cast-iron pan over medium-low heat, heat roughly 1 to 1½ inches of sunflower seed oil. Line a plate with paper towels and set aside. Cook the fishballs, turning until all sides are equally golden in color, about 3 to 5 minutes. Transfer the fishballs to a paper towel–lined plate and lightly salt to taste.

For the horseradish mayonnaise: Peel the horseradish and grate it into a small bowl using a Microplane. Add the mayonnaise and mix to combine well. Finish by adding pepper and stir again.

Serve the fishballs with the Horseradish Mayo alongside.

LAFAYETTE OR CARMINE?

Some people work or eat at both, but some wouldn't be caught dead at one or the other. There's no real rhyme or reason to taking a side. As much as people try to make it a rivalry, it simply isn't. It was like deciding between U2 or R.E.M.: a completely made-up feud that rock "enthusiasts" of the '80s and '90s like to think existed. Undoubtedly, both are great bands. This isn't Biggie v. 2Pac, East v. West.

When we opened in the West Village, the goal was for everything to be the same. Same placemats, same playlist, same menu—just sub Rose Water Waffles for Orange Blossom Pancakes—the stripes, the artwork, some familiar faces, the music, and of course, *the bell*.

Lafayette's bell was a gift from a friend and ex-coworker, Hans. It's a fire-engine red devil figure holding a chain. When you pull on its arm, the bell rings. The whole place can hear it. I mean it's *loud*. Even though it's in the back of the restaurant, one pull has fifty people looking up from their eggs. Obviously we look for any excuse to ring the bell. Curtis, a friend and artist whose work hangs on our walls, walking through the front door on a Tuesday gets quite the introduction. What better way to own up to dropping a glass than with a reverberating *DINGGG!* Newcomers treat the bell like a sacred object—"What's the bell for?" "Can I ring it?"—but this isn't church. You're eating peri peri chicken wings and the people next to you are probably taking pictures of you eating peri peri chicken wings. Don't take it too seriously. Just ring the damn bell.

A Jack's Wife Freda birthday wouldn't be a birthday without a bell ring. Whether it's the middle of brunch or late at night when the lights are dim, Dean will orchestrate dessert coming out of the kitchen like Michael Jackson coming out from the bottom of the stage. Lights off, three malva puddings with candles blazing emerge from the kitchen, the whole dining room singing "Happy Birthday" in unison, the entire parade ending with a gigantic bell ring. It's the cherry on top. Can you beat that, Batali? I don't think so. It's ridiculous, wild, and fun. We've made lots of new friends and impressed the old ones too.

A few weeks before Carmine was to open, I planned a quick trip to Rhode Island. I had worked like twelve days straight and was beat. Dean reminded me, "Carmine still needs a bell, you know." He knew it, I knew it. You're not finding the perfect bell in New York City; you're going to find it in Providence. And sure enough, I came back with a bell as weird as the last. Come by sometime and try ringing this one, too.

—Oliver Klein

FLOURLESS CHIPOTLE CHOCOLATE CAKE

Yields 1 10-inch cake/10 to 12 servings

In essence this dessert has more in common with a soufflé than a cake, but nonetheless it is a decadent end to a great meal. Try to find a good-quality semisweet chocolate that is at least 60 percent cocoa. Julia's addition of chipotle lends just a touch of spice to her signature recipe, which couples beautifully with the richness of the chocolate.

1 pound (4 sticks) butter

1 pound good-quality semisweet chocolate (at least 60% cocoa)

2 cups sugar

10 large eggs

½ teaspoon ground chipotle

Melt the butter in a microwave or a double broiler. If the chocolate is in bar form, chop it into small pieces, add the chocolate to the butter, and mix with a spatula until melted and completely smooth, making sure there are no bits of chocolate left.

In a large bowl, whisk the sugar, eggs, and ground chipotle until light and frothy. Slowly add the chocolate mixture to the eggs and mix until fully combined and the color is uniform.

Grease a 10-inch springform pan with baking spray and pour the batter into the pan. Refrigerate the cake for at least 30 minutes or overnight.

Preheat the oven to 300°F. Place the springform pan on top of a baking sheet. Place on the middle rack in the oven. Bake for 1 hour and 30 minutes. The cake will puff up, sometimes over the top of the pan; if this happens, carefully tuck the sides back into the pan once the cake has finished baking. The cake will fall naturally as it cools.

Let the cake set for at least 30 minutes before removing the sides of the pan. Note that the center of the cake will be set but still soft. Serve in small slices garnished with your choice of topping, such as whipped cream, fresh berries, or caramel.

NECTARINE AND PLUM FRUIT CRISP

Yields one 9-inch pie dish/8 to 10 servings

We change our crisp seasonally depending on what fruits are the ripest and most abundant. You can substitute any fruit in the recipe below. We're particularly partial to stone fruit season in late summer, so this nectarine and plum iteration is one of our favorites. Add a dollop of labneh and a drizzle of honey before serving.

4 nectarines

6 black or red plums

¾ cup packed brown or other preferred sugar

Zest and juice of 1 lemon

¾ cup plus 2 tablespoons flour

¾ cup rolled oats

1½ teaspoons ground cinnamon

¾ cup (1½ sticks) butter

Pinch of kosher salt

Use a 9-inch glass, ceramic, or metal pie dish to bake the crisp.

Preheat the oven to 350°F. Cut the nectarines and plums into wedges, discarding the pits. Add ½ cup of the brown sugar to the fruit and stir to combine. Add the lemon zest and juice and 2 tablespoons of the flour to the fruit and mix well. Let the fruit sit for a few minutes, then transfer to the pie dish, making sure to stir the fruit once before transferring.

In a small bowl, combine the remaining ¾ cup flour, the oats, remaining ¼ cup brown sugar, the cinnamon, and the salt. Using a pastry cutter or your fingers, work the butter into the flour mixture until it comes together and small pea-size lumps begin to form. Cover the fruit with the topping and refrigerate for 20 minutes. Put the pie dish into the oven on top of a baking sheet to catch any juices that overflow. Bake for 1 hour to 1 hour and 15 minutes, or until the topping is golden brown.

MALVA PUDDING

Yields 9 portions

This South African dessert of Cape Dutch origin is a dense cake soaked in a delicious caramel sauce. It can vary with the additions of ginger, apricot jam, and sometimes brandy or dates. Malva, which is Afrikaans for "marshmallow", describes the spongy texture and sweetness of this unique dessert. We bake our Malvas in a muffin tin for individual portions and serve them hot from the oven, with extra sauce drizzled on top and a spoonful of fresh whipped cream.

6 tablespoons (¾ stick) butter

3 large eggs

1 cup granulated sugar

1 teaspoon white wine vinegar

1 tablespoon plus 1 teaspoon vanilla extract

½ cup whole milk

1 cup flour

1 teaspoon baking soda

½ teaspoon kosher salt

1 cup heavy cream

¾ cup packed brown sugar

Whipped cream, for serving

Spray 9 cups of a standard metal muffin tin with baking spray. Preheat the oven to 325°F.

Melt 3 tablespoons of the butter and set aside. In an electric mixer, whisk the eggs with the granulated sugar until thickened and pale yellow. Mix the melted butter and vinegar together in a small bowl and add to the egg mixture. Add 1 tablespoon of the vanilla and ¼ cup of the milk to the mixture, whisking to combine.

In a separate bowl, mix the flour, baking soda, and salt. Add the dry ingredients to the wet and whisk to combine. Fill the prepared wells of the muffin tin three-quarters full and bake for 30 minutes.

While the cakes are in the oven, prepare the sauce. Combine the heavy cream, remaining 3 tablespoons butter, brown sugar, remaining ¼ cup milk, and remaining 1 teaspoon vanilla in a saucepan over medium-high heat. Bring to a boil, whisk, and remove from the heat.

Let the Malvas cool slightly, remove from the muffin tin, and place in a glass baking dish or another vessel able to comfortably hold them all, making sure the sides of the dish are tall enough to reach at least half the height of the cakes.

Using a skewer or toothpick, poke holes all over each Malva. While still hot, spoon sauce onto each pudding, going back multiple times until you've used all the sauce. Serve the Malvas warm with extra sauce from the bottom of the pan, spooned on top along with fresh whipped cream.

YOGURT PANNA COTTA WITH ROSE SYRUP

Yields six 4-ounce servings

This unfussy, elegant dessert can be prepared in a matter of minutes and requires only the stovetop and a few hours in the fridge. Greek yogurt gives this panna cotta a tart and sour flavor that is perfectly suited for the sweet rose syrup. We add pistachios for a crunch.

1 package gelatin (2¼ teaspoons)

2 tablespoons cold water

2 cups full-fat Greek yogurt

1½ cups heavy cream

¼ cup sugar

1 teaspoon vanilla extract

ROSE SYRUP

¾ cup sugar

2 tablespoons rose water

3 tablespoons pomegranate juice

½ cup shelled pistachios, coarsely chopped

Choose four glass ramekins or small shallow bowls to set your panna cotta in, and have them ready next to the stove.

Sprinkle the gelatin over the cold water in a medium bowl and let sit for 5 minutes.

In a large bowl, whisk the yogurt until it is smooth and set aside.

Bring the cream and sugar to a boil in a small saucepan; immediately remove from the heat.

Slowly add the hot cream mixture to the gelatin, whisking until smooth. In a steady stream, add the mixture to the yogurt and whisk until well combined and completely smooth.

Portion the panna cotta equally into four glass ramekins or shallow dishes, cover with plastic wrap, and refrigerate for at least 3 hours.

While the panna cotta is chilling, make the rose syrup: Combine the sugar, ¼ cup water, the rose water, and the pomegranate juice in a small saucepan and bring to a boil. Reduce the heat to a simmer and cook for 5 minutes. Transfer the syrup to a container to cool completely.

Once panna cotta is chilled, cover each with ¼ inch of the syrup and sprinkle with chopped pistachios. Rose syrup will keep, refrigerated, for up to 2 weeks.

ACKNOWLEDGMENTS

Deepest gratitude and appreciation to our editor, Sarah Hochman, for all you have done in finding us and believing in this book. Our thanks to everyone at Blue Rider Press and Penguin Random House.

For your support, help, and love: Brian Jankelowitz, Chad Jankelowitz, Ayelet and Asi Berman, Ron Krell and family, Steven Kamali, Henry Hargreaves, Tina Thor, Piper Perabo and Stephen Kay, Zohar and Yaniv Zohar.

To Maya's parents, Aviva Bachar and Michael Weiss, and Dean's parents, Rona Kahn and Brian Jankelowitz.

For being with us all along the way, listening to our dreams, and always believing: Galit Sharvit and David BenSadoun, Kara Baradarian, Anthony Lipschitz, Gavin B. Sclar and family, Amir and Nirit Weingarten, Michal Green Rubin.

To our chef, Julia Jaksic: Encountering Julia has been one of the rare treats in our life. For her understanding of who we are as a people, her uncanny interpretation of our favorite dishes, her love for everyone she works with, and her calming presence—thank you.

To Laureen Moyal and Mikey Pozarik, and the team at Paperwhite Studio for constant design brilliance and imagination; Sarah Tihany for your penmanship and friendship; Alessandra Olanow for illustrating Freda so whimsically; and to Patrick Hessert, a very special thank you.

To Yony Lopez, Erick Fernandez and our entire team in the kitchen. To our incredible service team who make it all possible every day, each and every one of you. To our partners, vendors, suppliers and of course to our guests—this book is for you.

To the teachers, friends, and family who have come across our paths.

To our precious boys, Noam and Bennie Jankelowitz, your presence is our inspiration.

—Maya and Dean Jankelowitz

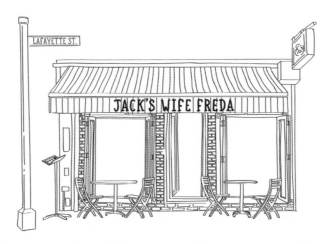

ACKNOWLEDGMENTS

Thank you to Dean and Maya for allowing me the creative freedom and inspiration to express myself through food.

To my husband, Erik, for his constant and dedicated support.

To our editor, Sarah Hochman, for her immense patience and understanding.

To Susan Weiss Berry for her guidance and direction.

To Dean and Sharon Bahrman for the use of their beautiful kitchen to test my recipes in.

To Yony, Erick, and the Jack's Wife Freda kitchen staff for their daily commitment to making each dish as beautiful as it can be.

To my family for their love and constant appetite.

To my Nana Anka for planting the culinary seed in me at such a young age, and teaching me the importance of family, nourishing others, and the joy of cooking.

—Julia Jaksic

INDEX

Veggie Curry with Apple-Raisin Chutney,
    182, 183

tomato juice, *in* Bloody Mary, *146, 147*

Tuna Salad, *100,* 101

Tzatziki, 20

V

Veggie Curry with Apple-Raisin Chutney,
    182, 183

vinaigrettes

Balsamic Vinaigrette, 101

Red Wine Vinaigrette, 97

Tarragon Vinaigrette, 95

W

Waffles, Rose Water, *56, 57*

watercress

Chicken Prego, *110,* 111

Pea and Ricotta Toast, *84, 85*

Smoked Paprika Egg Salad, *112,* 113

watermelon juice, *in* The Pink Guzzler,
    136, 137

Wessman, Luke, 69

wheat berries, *in* fall grain bowl, 120

whitefish, smoked, *in* Freda's Fishballs,
    198, 199

winter squash

fall grain bowl, 120

Mustard Seed–Crusted Tofu, *122, 123*

Y

yellow squash, *in* Vegetable (Veggie) Curry
    Bowl with Apple-Raisin Chutney,
    182, 183

yogurt

Grapefruit Yogurt, *40, 41*

Lebanese yogurt, about, 16

Potato Latkes with Apple-Cinnamon Yogurt,
    34, 35

Tzatziki, 20

Yogurt Panna Cotta with Rose Syrup, *212, 213*

Z

za'atar

Avocado Toast, *90, 91*

to make, 16

Spiced Beet Dip, *156, 157*

Spiced Rack of Lamb with Israeli Couscous,
    196, 197

zucchini

summer grain bowl, 120

Veggie Curry with Apple-Raisin Chutney,
    182, 183

Zucchini Chips, *160, 161*

DEAN AND MAYA JANKELOWITZ

are the co-owners of Jack's Wife Freda, the wildly popular

pair of identically named restaurants in New York City's

Greenwich Village and SoHo neighborhoods.

They have two children and live in downtown Manhattan.

JULIA JAKSIC

is a consultant on various restaurants in Manhattan and Brooklyn, and with the Jack's Wife Freda restaurants in SoHo and the West Village. She became the chef of Employees Only in 2006, and is currently the executive chef and consultant. Jaksic specializes in fresh, simple flavors and slow food cooking. She learned butchery from her father, who worked in New York's Meatpacking District in the 1970s. Jaksic lives in New York and Nashville, Tennessee.

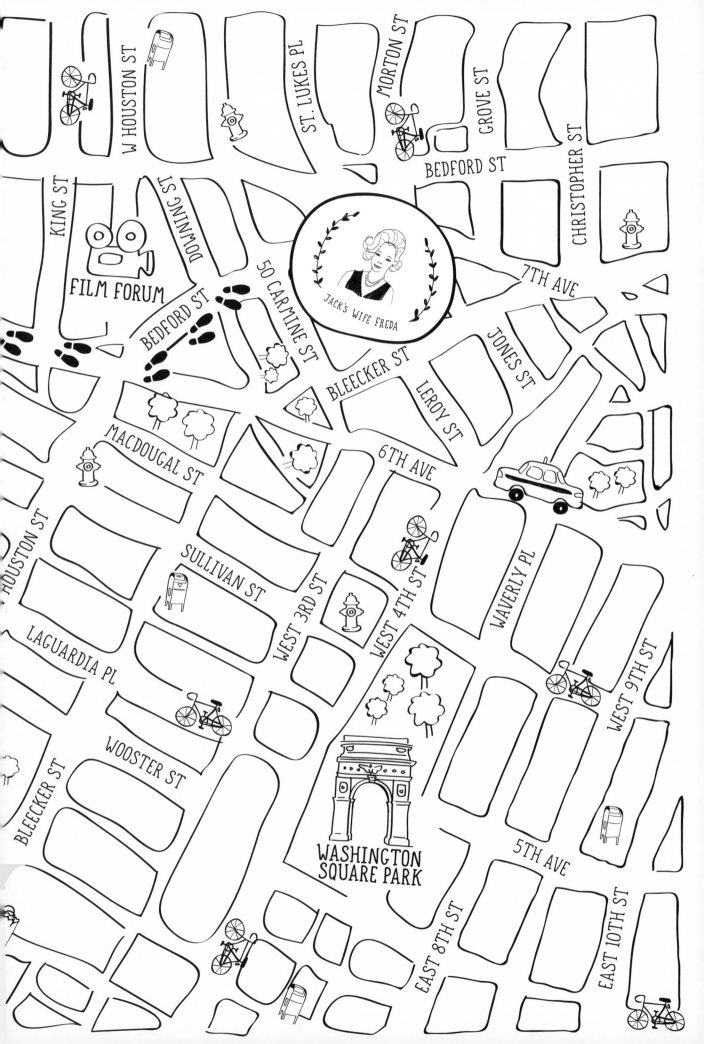

COME AND VISIT US SOMETIME

50 CARMINE STREET
between Bleecker and Bedford Streets
New York, NY

224 LAFAYETTE STREET
between Spring and Kenmare Streets
New York, NY